THE SCHOOL OF LIFE is dedicated to exploring life's big questions: *How can we fulfill our potential? Can work be inspiring? Why does community matter? Can relationships last a lifetime?* We don't have all the answers, but we will direct you toward a variety of useful ideas—from philosophy to literature, psychology to the visual arts—that are guaranteed to stimulate, provoke, nourish, and console.

THESCHOOLOFLIFE.COM

"In an age of moral and practical confusions, the self-help book is crying out to be redesigned and rehabilitated. The School of Life announces a rebirth with a series that examines the great issues of life, including money, sanity, work, technology, and the desire to alter the world for the better."

—ALAIN DE BOTTON,
THE SCHOOL OF LIFE SERIES EDITOR

About the Author

SUSAN QUILLIAM is a relationship psychologist, coach, advice columnist and faculty member of the School of Life. She is the author of twenty-two books published in thirty-three countries and twenty-four languages. She is a regular media expert on the subject of sex and relationships. For more information, please visit susanquilliam.com.

Also by Susan Quilliam

The Joy of Sex (cowritten with Dr Alex Comfort)

Stop Arguing, Start Talking

Staying Together

HOW TO CHOOSE
A PARTNER

HOW TO CHOOSE A PARTNER

Susan Quilliam

PICADOR

New York

HOW TO CHOOSE A PARTNER. Copyright © 2016 by The School of Life. All rights reserved. Printed in the United States of America. For information, address Picador, 175 Fifth Avenue, New York, N.Y. 10010.

picadorusa.com • picadorbookroom.tumblr.com
twitter.com/picadorusa • facebook.com/picadorusa

Picador® is a U.S. registered trademark and is used by Macmillan Publishing Group, LLC, under license from Pan Books Limited.

For book club information, please visit facebook.com/picadorbookclub or e-mail marketing@picadorusa.com.

Designed by Steven Seighman

The photographic credits starting on page 175 constitute an extension of this copyright page.

The Library of Congress Cataloging-in-Publication Data is available upon request.

ISBN 978-1-250-07869-8 (trade paperback)
ISBN 978-1-250-07870-4 (e-book)

Our books may be purchased in bulk for promotional, educational, or business use. Please contact your local bookseller or the Macmillan Corporate and Premium Sales Department at 1-800-221-7945, extension 5442, or by e-mail at MacmillanSpecialMarkets@macmillan.com.

Originally published in Great Britain by Macmillan, an imprint of Pan Macmillan

First U.S. Edition: January 2017

10 9 8 7 6 5 4 3 2 1

For Michael and Silvano. I could not wish for better friends.

Contents

—

1. Understanding

When you make a choice, you change the future.
(Deepak Chopra)

Choosing a romantic partner is one of contemporary life's biggest adventures. Embark on the quest and we may meet fascinating people as well as some who make us crazy; we may rise to emotional heights as well as sinking into fury, fear and depression; we may lose direction completely before at last we find our way to love.

The real challenge is that we grow. Partner choice is a self-development journey, driving us to learn more about ourselves, about other people, about life and the way we want to live it. Take all that on board and we start to realize just how big an adventure choosing a partner is.

What we may not realize is just how much bigger and more difficult that adventure is now more than ever before in history. For up to now, humankind has been sensible about partner choice. Of course lust and romance have had much to do with it – especially around affairs, liaisons or simple flings. But for serious lifetime

The Arnolfini Portrait by Jan van Eyck, a celebration of uber-traditional marriage with one main aim – an heir.

pairing, people have historically leaned away from the romantic and towards the pragmatic. The rich have typically chosen a partner for honour, for fortune, for political expediency and to preserve the hereditary line. The less rich – with less to protect – have had more leeway to let hearts rule heads, but have still needed to guarantee financial security, secure practical support and bear children to provide for later years.

Even in the glorious Age of Chivalry, when a knight's love for his lady was a key life aim, no one ever suggested that romance should lead to commitment; in the Court of King Arthur, Lancelot and Guinevere's real crime was not so much in adoring each other as in trying to make their adoration the basis for a 24/7 relationship. As historian Stephanie Coontz points out in *Marriage, a History*, while people have always enjoyed a love story, up until very recently 'our ancestors didn't live in one'.

An emotional revolution

Fast forward to the twentieth century and romance became an imperative. Claire Langhamer, in her book *The English in Love*, explains that this emotional revolution had been simmering for a while, but was fully triggered into being by many and varied social changes – though who knows which of these was cause and which effect. The introduction of the contraceptive Pill making partnerships less focussed on procreation and more on emotional connection? Women becoming more educated, more highly paid and therefore more able to exit loveless marriages? The slaughter of two World Wars encouraging us to seize the day and prioritize short-term intensity over long-term commitment? The rise of social liberalization, mass education, global communication? The fall in religious belief, the rise of individual entitlement, the passing of divorce laws?

Whatever the reasons, somewhere around the mid years of the last century, partnership became universally and inextricably linked with love. And that has tossed all the jigsaw-puzzle pieces into the air. For the first time, passion – sexual and emotional – has become the primary benchmark for relationship success. Think of the famous opening line of Jane Austen's *Pride and Prejudice*: 'It is a truth universally acknowledged, that a single man in possession of a good fortune must be in want of a wife.' Then compare that with the 1949 pronouncement by Rev. Herbert Gray, chair of the National Marriage Guidance Council, that 'the only sufficient reason for marrying is that you . . . love somebody . . .' Where matrimonial ads in the mid-1900s – when my own mother was making her partnership decisions – marketed prospective mates on their cleanliness, honesty and weekly wage, our contemporary equivalent, online dating sites, now trumpet the glories of 'Chemistry', 'Encounters' and being 'Soulmates'.

Reality hits

All of which sounds enticing. But the reality's more problematic. For we now approach partner choice with bigger expectations, deeper confusion and heavier pressure than ever before. Blending love into the relationship mix may have promised fulfilment but it's created huge challenges.

The first issue is that we need to make more choices more often. Centre-staging love means we're likely to want to walk away from a relationship if the romance dies, while less insistence on marriage plus more liberal divorce laws means we can do so far more easily. The result is that we now have not just one window of partner choice at biological maturity – with an additional window if a spouse dies – but on average five windows through a lifetime. We may choose in our teens for first love, in our twenties for first commitment, in our thirties for parenting partnership, in our forties for post-divorce companionship, with a final choice for relationship support to take us through to death. All that plus any additional liaisons.

Now set this increased need against decreased opportunity. We meet fewer partners because we are more globally mobile; as never before we move house, change jobs, relocate to new countries. We have less chance to create partnerships because we work long hours – then travel home, in different directions, to socially isolated conurbations. Plus, we're less resourced to find and choose a partner because we're less supported; we take the practical and emotional burden on our individual shoulders far more than when we only had to decide between marrying the boy/girl next door or the one further up the street. The final outcome of this blend of more demand and less supply? Meeting a mate has rarely been so challenging.

Happy endings?

And rarely so important. As never before, loving coupledom is now regarded as the key task of the human lifetime, and even more vital because we live in a fractured and isolated society. Cue that wise verse in Genesis where God says 'it is not good for man to be alone'.

Which leads us to another problem. For now, religion has less and less place in loving relationships, just as it has in the human psyche, to the point where not only is God absent from partnership but partnership has become more significant than God. Philosopher Simon May, in his book *Love: A History*, explains that where once we sought meaning in the divine, now that we can no longer find such meaning, we seek it elsewhere. Partnership is the source which is now expected to deliver all the hope and happiness that we originally expected to get from the deity.

Now, when we commit to someone, we're seeking a God-substitute – which means they have to be perfect. Then we have to become perfect God-substitutes for them, offering unconditional, everlasting and utterly selfless love. Coupledom has become not only a matter of

When you think about choosing a partner, do you envision a quest, a crusade, a battle, a treasure hunt . . . or a stroll in the park?

practical support, continuing the line or personal fulfilment; it's now the route by which
we gain sanctity and everlasting redemption.

Surely that's impossible? Well, of course it is.
Even in theory we can't reach the ideal expressed
by philosopher Friedrich Schlegel: 'through
love, humanity returns to its original state of di-
vinity'. And in practice we have regular proof of
how implausible that aim is. Proof in our own
imperfect relationships, proof in the daily media coverage of failed celebrity partnerships,
proof in the divorce figures that over recent
years have reached 70 per cent in some European
countries – and that doesn't include the endings
of unmarried, therefore undocumented, relationships.

Is it any wonder we panic about commitment? Traditional 'one time' selection limited
our freedom, but once paired off we had the possibility of lifelong security, and a near-guarantee
that if we stayed the course, society would call it
a win. Now we fear that if we choose wrong, we
will end up not only alone but condemned –
even damned – for our failure to make love
work.

If we ask older relatives what partner choice
was like for their generation, and what content-

ment, as well as what constraints, they felt, we may be in for a surprise. Our ancestors may not have lived in a love story, but with lower expectations – both their own and their partner's – they may well have had more happy endings than we do.

New benefits

All that said, I'm hugely grateful to be living and loving today. For new order brings new benefits. Our partnerships are now our own, rather than those imposed on us by family or proscribed by community. More dating 'windows' throughout life means more go-rounds to discover which relationship decisions help us thrive. More arenas from which to choose mean more ways to find partnership outside traditional boundaries – across culture, belief, class and age range. More freedom to walk away if we pick wrongly means not being trapped for life in an unfulfilling half-death.

And the current challenges are gradually finding solutions. Increased need and decreased opportunity are being met by a battery of ways to meet potential partners. My mother and her generation didn't imagine using dating agencies or matchmakers, but nowadays they often represent the elite level of the partner-choice range. My grandmother and her generation had never heard of the now ubiquitous speed dating – though I suspect she would have found it all great fun.

Then there's new technology. In the past two decades the internet has extended choice from the few in one's 'village' to millions worldwide; has given us a plethora of extra ways to reach out to partners through websites, apps and social media; has transformed the courtship process – albeit with the downsides that any newly born innovation brings. The landscape of relationship decision-making has changed for ever; where in the early 1990s, 1 per cent of couples met through technology, now an estimated 33 per cent do and there are claims that by 2040 this number will reach an astonishing 70 per cent.

This enormous social shift is being supported by the development of new knowledge, new insights, new resources. My mother – who was a school teacher as well as an incredibly wise woman – often bemoaned the fact that 'how to love' was not on any classroom timetable; her wish is now reality, with the growing crop of relationship courses, workshops, coaching and counselling that has sprung up to meet the need. Love may never in history have been so challenging, but perhaps never before have we been so resourced to meet that challenge.

Starting the adventure

Which leads us neatly to this book. I come to write it not only through my experiences as a teacher, coach and writer on relationship issues – as well, of course, as what I've learned through my own partnership decisions – but in particular through my association with the School of Life. Over the years I've worked with them, we've become more and more aware of a huge iceberg of concern around relationship choice, a concern that reaches across all genders, ages and nationalities.

How to Choose a Partner is a guide to finding the right partner for you – though be warned, it's not a map, not a tip-list, not an action manual. Instead, it is a series of reflections drawing on psychology, philosophy, culture and ordinary human experience. The book's wisdom is the wisdom not only of the many professionals who have considered the decisions that we make about love, but also of the class participants I have taught and the coaching clients I have worked with.

The aim is to inform, enhance and support your own thoughts, feelings and insights. Each chapter offers a different perspective on the issues, encouraging you to look not only at where you are now, but also at how your past has informed your present, how your criteria for a relationship can be clarified and refined, and how to explore whether you and a particular partner could be right for each other. In particular, the exercises and tasks that are scattered through the book invite you to consider the route you are taking on your journey and, if necessary, adjust it – to find, recognize and commit to a relationship in which you will thrive.

Here is the first task, an initial question for you to consider. How do you fit into this contemporary relationship landscape? Where do you stand as regards the 'new deal' of partner choice? Do you see it as an exciting challenge or a hopeless task, a complex puzzle or a terrifying trial? You might want to complete the following sentence. 'When I think about choosing a partner, I feel/realize/wonder . . .' This simple exercise will tell you a great deal about your hopes, your fears, your attitudes, your feelings.

As you read on, a final optimistic thought. You are not alone. There are literally many millions of people out there who, like you, are looking for a deep connection. Like you, they have previously made the best decisions they could, given their circumstances and resources. Like you, they have sometimes suffered regrets and disappointment but are now once again wanting to love and to be loved. There are many options out there when you are ready.

And, as the quotation at the head of this chapter suggests, by exploring these options you create a whole new set of possibilities for yourself. By taking on the adventure of choosing a partner, you have the opportunity of changing your future for ever. Starting now.

2. Being Ready

All things are ready if our mind be so.
        (William Shakespeare, Henry V, Act IV,
                                Scene III)

It's very tempting to rush into love. It's very tempting to think we're ready to love because we want to – and there's nothing wrong with that wanting. But readiness to even look for a partner, let alone choose one, can be more complicated than it seems. Which is why this second chapter is something of an amber traffic light.

The first amber question to ask is this. Is now the right time to be seeking a committed relationship? There are many life situations, temporary transitions and extended periods where being single is essential. Perhaps our focus currently needs to flow inwards to ourselves because our energy needs to flow outwards – maybe to a demanding job, a sick parent (or child), a sudden life crisis. If so, though we may want the support of a relationship because we threaten to collapse without it, choosing a partner may actually be the last thing in the world we should be attempting. And not just because

partnership's arguably the second hardest challenge of a lifetime – the first is parenting, if
you're wondering – so it shouldn't be under-
taken while vulnerable. But also because, vulnerable, we may choose a mate simply as a
crutch; crisis over, life healed, that crutch may
be superfluous. Unfair to both parties.

There are also many life phases when being
single is enough – not because we are running
on empty but because we are fulfilled. It can be
a hugely enlightening exercise to list the people
close to you then list the things they give to you,
the things that enhance your life. Company,
conversation, common history – or that simplest
of support, a hug. Do this exercise and it may
gradually dawn on you that most if not all of
your needs are being met at the moment. If so,
you may opt to put partner choice on hold – or
choose a mate who fills the current gap even if
they don't offer the traditional 24/7 comprehen-
sive companionship.

Staying on amber

The next amber question is even more challenging. Is it ever the right time to be choosing a

partner? It's said that the best thing in life is to be happily partnered and the next best thing is to be happily single – but for some people the hierarchy's reversed. Some of us are entirely whole without additions, flourish better without distractions, are simply happier alone.

If you suspect you're more contented when single, consider – and not just as a passing thought – whether partnership may not be what you are meant to do with your life. The ideal of singledom is highly valued in many spiritual traditions less because of puritanism than because it frees us to follow our real vocation. The composer Robert Schumann, when he achieved his initial musical success, is said to have compared it to his forthcoming marriage in these words: 'I doubt if being a bridegroom will be in the same class with these first joys of being a composer . . . I now . . . marry the wide world.' If you are seeking a relationship only because it is what 'everyone' does, try on for size the possibility that you are not everyone. You are special and the best way for you to thrive may be to 'marry the wide world'.

Planning

For the rest of us there are still the practicalities to consider. Do we actually have room in our lives right now to hold down a committed relationship? The reality is that online dating, for example, will likely take up an hour each night – the equivalent of a working day each week for anything up to a year.

And once the search is over, life will be even more overextended. For love may be wonderful, but it demands time, space, energy and a willingness to accommodate. And while statistically our formal working hours at the start of the twenty-first century are apparently almost half those we endured at the start of the nineteenth, the additional claims on that time, space and energy – by family, friends, hobbies, housework, travelling, childcare, texts, email, Twitter, Facebook and the miscellaneous demands of living – are arguably double what they were a hundred years ago.

The extra sting in the tale is that the more successful we've been in life up to now, the more we've developed our career, expanded our social life and gained a rewarding lifestyle, the less room we have for partnership. The more established we are in our world, the less flexibility we have for allowing a partner into that world. To love, we may have to sacrifice at least some of the rest of our lives. (For moving stories from people who feel they've not sacrificed as they should have done, see the website www.notime forlove.com, which describes itself as a project to acknowledge that 'in a reality where time is finite, prioritizing love, in any form, can be challenging'.)

Try this exercise. Map out your typical week – morning, afternoon, evening. Indicate which of those twenty-one time segments are currently full to the brim, then judge how many segments you would – or could – happily drain in order to make room for a relationship. Then ask what having a relationship might drain from the rest of your life and what the rest of your life might drain from a relationship. Is the bargain worth it? This is not, you understand, to dissuade you from the journey, but to make the advance planning more realistic.

Facing fears

Which brings us to the question of emotional readiness. Here, the elephant in the room is

Stop? Go? Wait? Hesitate? Panic and stay pinned to the pavement?

typically the emotion of fear – particularly because choosing a partner also involves the in-
timidating challenge of being chosen.

When I ask the men and women in my dating
classes to think of one word to describe how
they feel about partner choice, what is mentioned
more than anything else is some variation on
the fear concept; unease, wariness, anxiety, terror. As well as fear of making the wrong
choice, we suffer fear of being rejected – 'I'm
too fat, too shy'; fear of being left on the shelf –
'I'm too old, too boring'; and fear of being
shamed by being left on the shelf, particularly
when our peers all seem to have clambered
down from said shelf and are now happily
mated. Though on that last point, be aware that
one never knows what goes on behind closed
doors. Not to encourage *Schadenfreude*, but
many of the couples who seem most happy now
will be the ones sobbing on your shoulder when
they hit their first divorce in a few years' time.

There's also huge fear of admitting the
fear. We don't want to confess – in this age of
self-possession – that we're struggling, that
we're not completely fine about the whole
partner-choice business. *Bridget Jones's Diary*
made us laugh at Bridget's dating struggles not

only because her errors redeemed ours but also because her fight for control over life and love made us more able to break the silence and admit our own struggle to ourselves and to others. And Bridget's final triumphant union with Mark Darcy, when it came, reassured us that there could be a good result even for those of us most petrified.

Since Bridget, many books – both fiction and self-help – have urged a 'fake it till you make it' attitude to fear. But there is another way. More recently, and to my mind more usefully, we've started to embrace the suggestion that vulnerability may be better than bravado. Writer Brenè Brown, in her book *Daring Greatly*, brings the fear story up to date when she talks about the huge courage it takes to even consider entering a relationship, let alone doing so – but how the act of revealing the fear behind that courage is a key first step on the road to successful partnership. This is vulnerability. This is 'daring greatly'.

Many of us already do just this. When my class participants confess their lack of self-confidence, I often look round the room awed by what these men and women are bringing to the field. Intelligence, personality, talent – but,

above all, the courage and willingness, often despite earlier heartbreak, to dare greatly once
again. Because of that, surely success is certain.
As the Chinese proverb says, 'Pearls don't lie on
the seashore. If you want one, you have to dive
for it.' And we do.

Available or not?

Being ready for love also depends not only on
being emotionally open but also emotionally
available. The crucial instance of this is that,
however long it is since our last relationship, if
we still grieve that story, if we secretly hope to
open up its pages again, we can't move on to our
life's next volume. Yes, it's common to believe
that a new romantic connection will begin a
new chapter. Scan the tabloid headlines and
we find numerous triumphal reports of newly
loved-up celebrities who underwent break-ups
just a few weeks ago. Scan the online dating
sites and we similarly discover the many profiles
saying 'We separated last week so now I'm keen
to find love again'.

But the assumption's unsound. Yes, humans
are wired to bond – but when a bond breaks, hu-

mans are doubly wired to suffer and that makes us unfit to bond again for a while. Helen Fisher, Professor of Anthropology at Rutgers University, MRI-scanned fifteen newly single students and found their brains shimmering with a pain akin to that of going cold turkey from drug addiction. So it's not surprising that post-break-up is rarely the moment when we are emotionally available to connect with another. Problem is, that's precisely the moment in which we may be driven to connect in order to dull the pain – but then, once the injury is healed, find ourselves looking at our newly acquired partner and wondering what on earth we just did.

So how long does it take after losing a love to be truly and wisely available again? There are no schedules here. For recovery after a break-up, the litmus test is whether we can yet think about our former partner kindly – or if not, then at least not with hate but with love's true opposite, indifference. The delightful blog quantified-breakup.tumblr.com – by a blogger herself in 'relationship recovery' – lists several calculations for this, from 'at least two years' through 'half the length of the relationship' to 'one week for every month you were together'.

When it comes to a variation on the theme

of losing a partner – bereavement – the schedule may be more protracted; Jeanette Winterson's downbeat but arguably accurate appraisal in her book *Written on the Body*, in which her heroine tries to come to terms with her lover's leukaemia, is 'To lose someone you love is to alter your life for ever.' Whatever the situation, the only definitive truth is that being ready for the next relationship will always take just as long as it takes.

Being grown-up

The final, tough-love question about readiness is this. Are we yet 'grown-up enough' to pick a partner? Mischievously, that very wording is a test; if we're willing to even consider the question, we're probably on the way to ready, for success in partner choice often lies in the ability to question ourselves with mature and undefended honesty.

On this point, we turn to philosopher and social psychologist Erich Fromm, whose master work, *The Art of Loving*, is arguably the seminal statement of our contemporary view of what love can and should be. Fromm outlines in detail what he sees as the supremely 'grown-up' task of partnering with another human being. In his view, mature partner choice needs the self-belief that we are worth loving, the self-insight to know what we need and the self-control to let go of our needs where necessary. Plus, the ability to teach a partner how to love us, the humility to learn from a partner how to love them and the insight to know that love doesn't just consist of partnership but constitutes, in Fromm's words, the 'only sane and satisfactory answer to the problem of human existence'. At which point, most of us will run screaming from the room, thinking that for this weight of responsibility we're not only unprepared right now but will always remain so.

Let's not panic. If we can realize that the 'art' Fromm speaks of is not one we're born with but one which, like any art, we learn, then the challenge becomes more manageable. Love is surely not a single act but an ongoing course of lessons. Which means that at this point, as we choose a partner, all we really need to ask ourselves is whether we're ready to fill in the enrolment form.

Of course, it isn't only we who need to be ready for love, but also the partner we choose.

So it's more than a good idea to also do due diligence on a potential partner's readiness. We're not talking here about the relentless first-date quizzing that makes the person on the other side of the restaurant table reach for the bill after the first course, but a compassionate awareness of whether the person we are beginning to care for is truly free. Do they have time and room in their life for love? Are they over their past relationship or actually still yearning? Are they reaching out to us through genuine attraction or to fill a life gap?

If the answer to any of these questions is 'unclear', we may be wiser to step back and allow them the time and space they need. And allow ourselves to find a partner more ready to be chosen.

3. Looking Back

Study the past if you would define the future.
                                        (Confucius)

When we actively search for a long-term partner, most of us tend to think ahead. We map
out goals. We create aims. And the more serious a partnership we want, the further ahead we
tend to think – not just to meeting a new date,
but to moving in, to getting wed, to which gender our first child will be. There's wisdom in
that. To choose well we have to gauge what the
long-term will deliver.

But there's wisdom too – as Confucius says –
in first putting attention back to the past. How
has it made us who we are? What does that
mean for who we choose? It's not only that our
past partnerships have been preparation for this
moment, giving us both ability and vulnerability around loving. It's also that every event in
our past – from the moment we were born, let
alone from the moment we began to date – has
taught us messages about partnership and partnership choice. Whom we choose may be our

decision alone, but why we choose will be influenced by a whole lifetime's cast of characters and scenes.

Your influences

It's an interesting exercise to look back at our personal cast-list and our personal life-plot. Was it our mother, father or neither who taught us, by what they said or what they did, which kind of relationship we should aim for and which we should avoid? Was it our siblings, our friends, our teachers or our culture that told us we should choose a partner for their intelligence, their earning power, their beauty or their biddability? Was it being brought up in a conflict-ridden family or being a member of the debating society that has made us believe so completely that perfect partners either never argue or that, conversely, they regularly do? Is it our parents' ruby wedding anniversary or our own recent relationship break-up that leaves us convinced either that love lasts for ever or that it is utterly impossible? And what role do Jane Eyre, James Bond, *Fifty Shades of Grey* or *The Selfish Gene* have in all this?

So review. Who have been your biggest influencers on how best to choose a partner? What has most shaped your thoughts and feelings about the kind of person who will be the best mate for you?

- Parents, siblings, extended family
- Religious or cultural leaders, teachers
- Your peer group and their partners
- Your past loves, requited or unrequited
- The media, be that news, books, films, the internet, television
- Traumatic events in your own life or the lives of those close to you
- Positive, affirming events in your own life or the lives of those close to you

Now take this further. Consider what messages all of these have passed on to you. What definitions, expectations and presuppositions have you learned about the kind of relationship you should want, and so what kind of partner to pick? It may help to complete the following sentence: 'I learnt from ____ that the best relationship is ____ and so I should choose a partner who ____', and to complete that sentence at least ten times to get a range of differing messages. Then, see if there are any patterns, any surprises, any wake-up calls. Most crucial, how have these life lessons affected the partner choices you've made up to now?

Love maps

For more insight let's turn to sexologist John Money, who calls these lessons 'love maps' – templates of how we see ideal partnership and how we see our ideal partner. Money suggests that we gain love maps instinctively and early – often between the ages of about five and eight – as if we're picking up an accent in our native language. So we don't question, perhaps hardly even notice, the internal image we're building of relationships, the specifications we're drawing up about the kind of partner we want – often down to race, height, build and manner. When we find someone fitting that map, we're compelled. Yes, we may know on a logical level that an alternative mate may be just as good for us; but somehow this person just feels right.

Very often, the person feels right because they remind us of someone who felt right ear-

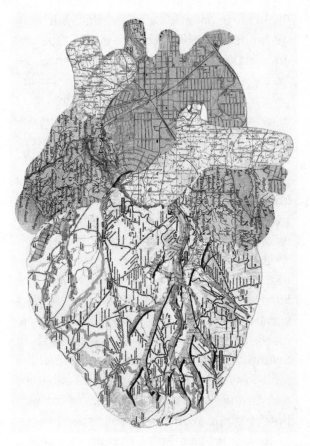

Navigating one's way through the highways and byways of the
heart can take concentration, courage and an accurate road map.

lier in life or because we believe that with them we can reclaim the 'right' life events. One way of describing this would be 'transference'; we 'transfer' affection from someone who was important to us in the past to someone important to us now – or to someone we want to be important to us in the future. A tone of voice, a sideways glance, a certain strength, a certain gentleness – all of a sudden, typically without knowing why, we feel we're safe. No matter that we don't know this person and they don't know us; we feel inevitably drawn in.

It makes absolute sense to gravitate to the people most like the ones who have made us happy in life, and much of the time that's a wonderful strategy. But get expectations confused, and it can go wrong. We can end up assuming a prospective partner will deliver the same kind of wonderful experiences that our parents (or our best school friend, or our very first 'crush') gave us. But partners don't necessarily deliver, because they're not that person and this isn't the past – realizing this and accepting it is a key lesson of partner choice. Professor Sue Johnson tells how when she met her husband almost the first words he said to her were, 'I am not going to live up to your expectations'.

In the face of such insight how could she do anything other than marry the man?

Think back to when you were very young – say just starting school. Now identify three figures – perhaps parents, teachers, siblings – or events – successes, wins, triumphs – that at that period in your life made you feel deeply valid and loved. You'll not only consciously look for a partner who holds out the promise of replicating those feelings but also be unconsciously drawn to any potential partner who holds out that promise. Good idea, with just one caveat. You may also be drawn to any partner you *believe* can deliver, even if they can't. So try before you buy.

Bad experiences

There's an added twist and it's this. Sometimes we get drawn to partners not because they could give us something wonderful but because they could give us something terrible – in the hope that they may also give us the chance to overcome that terror. So we may choose someone who reminds us how withdrawn our father was or how dominating our mother was, someone who creates demanding situations that remind us of exam failure in school or the time we got made redundant from work. We find all this painful but familiar, troubling but known; we aim, this time, to resolve, to cope, to survive.

And it often comes good. Often, we get to turn things round, to cope with challenges in later life in a way we didn't in earlier life because we are now older and wiser. And the fact that we cope not only gives us victory here and now, but helps to resolve the previous sense of failure. The Israeli poet Yehuda Amichai wrote that 'people use each other as a healing for their pain' – but in this case we are actively choosing each other for the pain, in hopes of getting the healing as part of the package.

Again, think back to your early life. Which people or events made you feel unloved or taught you hard lessons about what it means to relate to others? Do these memories link to your adult partners and the experiences you have had with them? What does that tell you about your partner-search strategies?

There is also, of course, the impact of life events so traumatic that they create a deep vulnerability in us, so we end wary, grief-stricken, furious or in some way simply too wounded to

make good partnership decisions. We may be
confused about what love means, unable to recognize it when it happens, unresourced to take
it when offered or give it when needed. The
obvious – and publicized – traumas are bullying,
abuse and violence, but other seemingly less
serious occurrences can wound us too. If our
world rocks on its axis – perhaps from a house
move, a hospital stay, an absent parent – we can
end up thinking love will let us down. If as a
child the only way we got any attention was
when we were punished for bad behaviour, we
may end up prone to tantrums in our relationships. The shock has not only broken our spirit,
but dented our capacity to make good partner
decisions.

Moving on

All the above works both ways. For our partners
too the 'past is prologue', as Shakespeare wrote,
and what happened in a partner's life before the
scenes they write with us affects not only who
they are but also who they are *when with us*.
Partners steer their course by their own love
maps, make their own transferences, have their

own stream of negative or traumatic characters
and episodes from their own lives. So they may
choose us because our ways of being wonderful
remind them of wonderful people and events in
their past, or because our ways of being difficult
remind them of difficult people and events in
their past. They too may need to align their expectations, to work through the difference between their hallucination and the reality that is
us – and to cope when we deliver the pain that
they unconsciously wanted to resolve through
being with us. If a partner seems to be reacting
in a way that says more about their history than
about the present reality of our relationship, it's
worthwhile paying close attention.

It is not all bad news. Though it's tempting
to believe that everything that comes to us from
the past is detrimental, it's not so. Normal, kind,
human love from those around us – whether
given in childhood or in adulthood – not only
provides us with solid ground for loving but
goes a long way to redress any harm that comes
our way. And while single intense experiences
of betrayal can wound us, similar experiences
of happiness, acceptance, success and security
can emotionally vaccinate us against mistakes.
For most of us, past bad experiences are not a

car crash on the relationship road, but simply a bump on the way.

Plus, we don't have to bring the past with us into the present. We can keep the bits that seem more helpful and most healthy; the others we can throw overboard. To which end, you may want to look back at all the lessons you've ever learned about love. Which messages are horribly outdated and need to be junked? Which are irrelevant to you now you're a grown-up? Which messages are so idealistic or perfectionist that no one has the slightest chance of matching up to them, and by continuing to try to match up, you are simply feeding your guilt monkey? Which were taught to you by people whose experience is not yours, whose word you no longer believe, or whose life you have no intention of living? Which lessons did you learn through events that were so painful that you need to cull them from your memory bank?

We can cull. With new awareness we can unbelieve our past beliefs, let them go and take on board a new and more helpful set. And if we can't do that alone, it's entirely possible – and utterly wise – to get help; there is a wealth of knowledge and guidance to help us overcome relationship issues. So if you suspect that some events or people have left you vulnerable to wrong choices or misguided decisions, let me encourage – even beg – you to see a professional. We can't change the life we've lived, but we can rethink it, understand it differently and so resolve the pain.

Confucius said that the past needs to be studied in order for us to define the future. Once studied, though, we may want to complete the lesson and move on.

4. Not Choosing

I believe marriages would in general be as happy, and often more so, if they were all made by the Lord Chancellor, upon a due consideration of characters and circumstances, without the parties having any choice in the matter.

(Attributed to Samuel Johnson, Boswell,
The Life of Samuel Johnson)

If you agree with Samuel Johnson, you're in a minority. Most people deeply believe that the best life outcomes are created by active and informed decisions. More, that if we ourselves don't make those decisions, we give up the chance of those best outcomes; we surrender control, cede responsibility and in so doing resign ourselves to compromise – as well as tacitly admitting that we're not up to the task of managing our own lives.

But let me argue the opposite. Maybe Johnson is right, and letting go of choice is a good idea. It's not just that love is one of the few areas in modern society where we may still cling to romantic notions of fate determining our future. But also, by handing over control to others, we might avoid repeating past mistakes or making new and future ones. When dealing with 'winged Cupid painted blind', as Shakespeare put it, taking our own blind prejudices out of the equation may be no bad thing.

Heads or tails?

Opt to step back from active decision-making, and the first possibility open to us is to toss a coin. When it comes to deciding a lifelong commitment, doing that literally may not seem wise, though devotees of the I Ching might disagree. A friend of mine did once use the system to decide whether to marry her boyfriend; the coins said 'no', which in hindsight proved to be excellent advice. And in Luke Rhinehart's *The Dice Man* – as its title suggests, a novel about a man who makes all choices thus guided – several partner-decisions are made that way. The result is whole-scale erotic abandonment under the absolving aphorism 'Who am I to question the dice?'

Let's consider next the American psychologist Barry Schwartz, whose work focusses on the reasoning behind choice. His argument is that randomness is a 'good enough' option. Once certain standards are met – we like each other well enough, we have similar life goals, we've checked issues such as substance abuse and criminal record – there are really no good reasons to discriminate between one suitor and the next. Chance, Schwartz suggests, might well be the 'most efficient' but also the 'fairest . . . most honest' option.

Interesting ideas, though most of us are wary of making key life decisions with so little information. Which is why I don't advise either coin-tossing, dice-throwing or absolute randomness. But I do suggest that to circumvent our biases and introduce a little serendipity, daters should, online, approach one random person in every twenty profiles they access, and offline be open to the occasional blind date, opportunity dinner from a colleague or fortuitous encounter at the supermarket checkout. Randomness certainly can open a different, less blinkered and therefore sometimes better door.

Destiny vs growth

The issue of fortuitous encounters brings us to an interesting double standard here. We may recoil in horror at the thought of haphazard chance determining our future life partner, but label that chance 'destiny' and we're entranced by the prospect. On the one hand we feel the need to be in control of our romantic choices; on the other hand the thought of losing control can be hugely seductive.

Enter Professor 'Chip' Knee of the University of Houston, and his work on 'destiny love', his term for the conviction held by some couples that kismet rather than coincidence brought them together. Believe this, and we are likely to feel strongly and instantly attracted to a partner, the relationship is likely to be passionate and intense, and a magical certainty of success is likely to hover over the whole enterprise. As a perfect example, see that scene in the film *Sleepless in Seattle* where Sam Baldwin describes meeting his first wife, speaks so movingly of taking her hand to help her out of a car, and – just with that initial touch – realizes 'we were supposed to be together . . . and I knew it.'

Sam Baldwin was lucky – thanks to a good scriptwriter creating the traditional rom-com happy ending – his ensuing marriage worked well. But the 'destiny' assumption may not survive the cold light of real-life daily commitment, because it comes with certain built-in structural defects. The problem is, if fate has generously provided us with a predestined partner, there may seem no need for effort to make the relationship work – and if effort is needed then that particular romance is clearly not as predestined as we thought it was and probably needs to end forthwith. Professor Knee's work suggests that those who believe in destiny love are likely to react badly when things go wrong, likely to exit relationships lightly, likely to move on quickly – to their next destiny.

Compare and contrast couples convinced of what Knee calls 'growth love', who see partnerships as developing slowly over time, with any glitches along the way meaning nothing sinister, but simply indicating a need for more effort. Growth-love couples tend to get involved more gradually, have lower expectations, but are more capable of the long haul. It is certainly worth remembering that while belief in fate-determined love – whether on our side or on a partner's – might add a breathless magic to romance, belief in growth-based love might mean the difference between a ruby wedding anniversary and being left at the altar.

Arranged

Letting destiny decide partner choice may seem like giving away control, but at least destiny (or fate or God or Providence) is all-seeing, all-knowing and infallible. Letting other, all-too-human beings decide partner choice seems a far worse bet, for ordinary folk are all too capable of confusion, ignorance, error and their own personal prejudices. Which is why, while accepting support on partner choice from friends and family may be helpful, it's usually better to block one's ears and step away. 'You should' and 'you must', even when voiced by onlookers with the best of intentions, should not govern partner decisions.

What does have a place, and a long history of some success – it's even mentioned in the Bible – is allowing others to 'arrange' possibilities which we can veto, or from which we make our own pick. Don't forget that until very recently, especially if a partnership was the way to cement political alliance or unite feuding families, it made perfect sense for elders rather than the happy couple to make the courtship decisions. In Britain, for example, it is only the last two generations of the monarchy that have had any kind of genuine personal freedom over marriage choice. (When certain of those love marriages failed, there was in some quarters a general feeling of 'Well, what did they expect?')

If done well, 'arranged' can triumph, delivering the objectivity of chance, the reassurance of destiny, the pragmatism of growth. Like chance, an externally determined partnership can avoid personal bias or the temptation to let lust dictate terms. Like destiny, it can remove the burden of choice, allowing us to relax rather than agonize about our own responsibility. Like growth love, 'arranged' can mean we don't demand instant compatibility, or call foul if things don't prove perfect always and for ever.

But there does need to be a high level of competence here. Matchmakers – whether they be friends, family, the Jewish *Shadchanim* or the upmarket urban introduction service – need to know us at least as well as we know ourselves, need to know our partners well enough to judge

"You're going to marry this n

Let us be grateful we don't live in 1917. Herbert Rawlinson and Alice Lake in the one-hundred-year-old black-and-white film *Come Through*.

Come through!"

"ght now – Come through!"

the fit, and need to have a deep understanding
of how relationships play out. The problem is
that this level of wisdom is unusual in today's
society. Few people witness others profoundly
and consistently enough to judge what is needed
in a mate. Few relationships are sufficiently
exposed to public gaze to deliver a real understanding of partnership dynamics. Which is
why, though popular, modern matchmaking
services can be infamous for high prices but low
results. That said, in the right context and if the
arranger is insightful and practised, 'arranged'
can work well.

A quick note on the extreme of 'arranged',
those serried ranks of mass marriages where
hundreds of couples meet for the first time on
their wedding day, their partner choice made
entirely by religious leaders. For most of us, this
is somewhere between incomprehensible and
appalling; how on earth does it ever work? The
answer is that spouses' contentment with the ar-
rangement is constructed on their deep belief
that they have the blessing of the deity; that their
culture, community, family and religion will
support them; and that love grows over time
rather than instantly strikes. Despite individual

horror stories, that's a pretty big resource to bring to the table.

Online choice

Does online dating take control out of our hands? At first glance, no; we seem to have a multitude of options. But look more closely and we see that what we get is pre-sorted. Most sites cherry-pick attractive users and profile them on the home page to catch incomers' attention. Many sites also highlight profiles of particularly popular users and present them as a separate and therefore more noticeable subcategory. We're getting a choice, but only after the site filters have done their secret work.

And then there are the algorithms. It was way back in 1959 that a group of Stanford University maths students working on a final class project programmed their IBM 650 computer to pair up forty-nine men and forty-nine women according to their answers to a questionnaire; the result was one marriage and a deserved A-grade for the dissertation. More than half a century on, and that early study has led to a billion-dollar industry; almost every online dating site has a visible 'questionnaire' and they all have hidden algorithms to guide us firmly towards matches of our age, location and gender of preference. Choice is, if not taken out of our hands, at least slightly compromised.

There's also another problem: dating sites only do the top level of the job. Yes, most sites match those who, on tick-box criteria, are similar, which replicates the surface-level criteria that attracts us to a mate; some sites then aim for more, with personality questionnaires or hormone-based matching systems. But while these matching systems maintain that the criteria for compatibility are well-established and that it's therefore possible to predict relationship success, in fact 'neither of these assumptions is true'. (I quote here from a recent research review of studies of online love-search by Professor Eli Finkel of Northwestern University, Illinois.) By allowing sites to try to match us, we are not only limiting our own options, not only failing to take into account the deeper compatibility factor, but also entrusting our fate to completely unproven systems.

Trusting chance

I'm not suggesting that abandoning choice altogether is either a good or a bad idea. But it is a possibility. What you may find useful is to think about what degree of abandonment you've used in the past without even realizing it. Have you ever started chatting to someone near you at the theatre, during a party, on a train – then spent a delightful half hour even though that didn't lead to romance? Probably. Have you ever met a partner by chance, circumstance or sheer happy coincidence? Again, probably. Have any of your intimate relationships been 100 per cent predetermined and predicted? Probably not. Start to gauge the extent to which you're comfortable with serendipity and you may feel more inclined to accept it as another tool in your decision-making kit.

Coin-tossing, random chance and a belief in fate are all quite risky. But handing over some of the burden to others is certainly worth considering – so perhaps let online dating sites screen the undesirables or let matchmaking services do the legwork. Allowing ourselves to widen our initial love-search beyond our personal preference is also useful – so perhaps

From time to time, they both wondered what the next forty years of marriage would bring.

make a deliberate effort to contact (or start talking to, or agree to a date with) someone who on the surface doesn't seem like a possible. Gathering emotional support is vital to get us through the process – so perhaps actively enrol trusted friends and turn to them for guidance, consolation and celebration.

Above all, when it comes to choice, be prepared to occasionally take a risk, accept uncertainty, let go of control. As ex–US president Jimmy Carter once said, 'Go out on a limb. That's where the fruit is.'

5. Focussing

Focus is about saying No.

(Steve Jobs)

Surely the more options we have, the more chance we have for love. Especially if we blame previous romantic disappointments on a lack of alternatives, then richness and variety of choice seem the obvious keys to success. Which is why the first question we may be asking about our love-search is how to find 'more' possibilities.

This is a great question if we're short on options, if our circle of single contacts has dwindled to nil; if we live in a town – or country – where we know no one; if we're not meeting any potential partners either at work or at play. It's an especially useful enquiry if we are in a majority gender for our life-stage: research suggests that men in their twenties have only half as many partner possibilities as women do, but that in the forties the balance begins to reverse. If we can't find a partner in these situations, the main problem is certainly the numbers. We're a seller in a buyers' market and the solution is to find more buyers.

The way forward is to steer clear of babbling brooks, avoid stagnant pools and find slow rivers. Stripped of the metaphors, what I mean is this: stay away from gatherings with no chance of 'get-to-know-you' conversations, or where meeting up again is unlikely. Don't get trapped in a social life where you see the same people over and over again. Instead, put your energy into groups which offer a steady and regular through-flow of different individuals, in situations where there's opportunity to mingle, meet, chat and bond. That's a slow river, and so long as it contains people with a similar background, outlook, values – it will deliver partner possibilities. Just as important, it will also deliver a fulfilled and fascinating existence as a base camp from which to embark on the partnership climb.

Finding a slow river

How many slow rivers do you have in your life? If the answer is not many, and getting 'more' is your issue, pause now and brainstorm what

Stagnant pools. It's worryingly easy to create a life so pleasant, established and secure that it delivers absolutely zero chance of meeting any suitable partner.

your rivers could be; include as many ideas as possible, without censoring even the maddest thoughts. Start a new hobby? Go to a partnered dance class? Attend dating events? Organize your own dating events? Put a call out on Facebook? Put a call out on your local radio station – it worked for Sam Baldwin, aforementioned hero of *Sleepless in Seattle*. Take off on a three-country tour – it worked for Elizabeth Gilbert, author of *Eat, Pray, Love*.

Plus – if it feels comfortable – sign up to a dating website. Whether we like it or not, online is without question the most accessible slow river currently available – one in which the whole agenda is to bond and the entire process ensures a regular through-flow. To enhance the expansion project, join a variety of sites – some paid, some free, some new, some established. Once on, be open-minded about possibilities, proactive rather than reactive and as flexible as possible about non-essential parameters. (Though not foolishly flexible. Tick the '200 miles away' location box on websites and you'll very soon face the reality of long-distance relationships and find yourself switching the location specification to 'same town'.)

More or less?

Having noted the above strategies, and taken the first steps towards action, forget the advantages of 'more' and embrace the benefits of 'less'. And not only because quantity is less crucial than quality in partner choice, but also because the human brain treads a fine line between having a wide range of options and having too many for sanity.

In a famous experiment by Professor Sheena Iyengar of Columbia University, customers at a grocery store decided what jam to buy; of those who had a choice of twenty-four jams, only 3 per cent ended up purchasing, while of those who had a choice of six jams a full 30 per cent bought. Given we likely don't use the same criteria to pick a partner as to pick a preserve, let's also mention a less-famous but more relevant survey which gave parallel results. Prospective partners who looked at either four or twenty-four online profiles made more picks than those who looked at sixty-four. Significantly, the participants who were presented with only four options took time to consider everyone, while those who were presented with twenty-four or sixty-four options made only cursory decisions.

If only choosing a partner were as simple as walking into a
supermarket. On the other hand . . .

The point here is that too many options plunges us into what's called 'shopping mentality'. With a profusion of possibilities, we suffer mental overload. We get confused. Then we get anxious about getting confused. And then, to combat the increasing emotional paralysis resulting from that confusion, we try to simplify. Which in turn leads to our over-considering irrelevant criteria, rejecting without real consideration, and craving the 'next good thing' rather than focussing on the current one. (This last is part of the reason why the constant forward momentum of the left/right swipe on some dating apps is so addictive.) Finally, when it comes to online dating in particular, even if we think we've found The One, we may still suffer buyer's remorse because the wealth of choice available suggests there's someone even better out there for us. If you've ever been enthusiastically emailed for days then suddenly dropped, you were probably the victim not of someone's rejection but of their shopping mentality.

What all this means is that any website which trumpets – as one of the global players did very recently – an astounding 197 million members might seem like a magnificent opportunity, but may well prove a disaster in disguise. Our real challenge, offline as well as on, is not how to expand possibilities but how to limit them, how to reach an equilibrium where we think clearly enough to make good judgement calls.

Elimination

The solution here is, not coincidentally, to take the route that nature intended. Intelligent elimination – the kind of shedding that Steve Jobs refers to in the quote at the head of this chapter – is the way evolution means us to mate. Walk into a room full of a hundred possibles – or log on to a website of a million – and we're doing just as our ancestors did thousands of years ago from the vantage point of their caves, unconsciously excluding those who don't meet our basic criteria (right gender, right age, right tribe). Elimination may sound cruel, but it's the way our instincts are meant to operate in the initial going – not saying 'yes' to one but 'no' to many, not making a single positive choice but first applying wholesale negative screening.

In a society more complex than the Neolithic, some screening's done before we even begin. Dive into any 'slow river' where we feel at home – a study group, a sports association, a dance course – and it's likely the event organizers have already aimed their publicity to eliminate people not in the tribe; we then informally cut the field by choosing to attend only certain events and then to mix only with certain people in the room.

Online, the system's parallel. From the start, some elimination's already done for us because we enter a world where those not looking for love have already self-excluded; many sites also helpfully (though covertly) screen out those with relationship-threatening issues such as drug abuse or long-term mental illness. We further narrow the range ourselves by signing up to sites that target our tribe even more specifically; there are now dedicated destinations for specific age groups, individual cities and almost any special interest you can name, along with some you can't even imagine.

Once signed up, the site tick-boxes create further focussing on surface compatibilities such as smoking (or not), drinking (or not), whether we follow sport or how passionately we love Chinese food. The algorithmic 'matching quizzes', if well done, then disqualify on deeper issues – though of course they can't predict face-to-face chemistry, and, as mentioned earlier, there's little correlation with long-term compatibility. Happily, the recent introduction of categories for 'serious', 'fling' or 'affair' now also achieves the elimination of those wanting a relationship of a kind we're not seeking, which is a huge relief for all those online daters single and looking for marriage who – up to a few years ago – kept bumping into those married and looking for a fling.

The funnel of love

All this pre-sorting is helpful. But the bottom line is that, however small the partner pool we fish in, there'll come a time when we need to do our own, more individual eliminations, partner by partner. My favourite metaphor here is one offered by the late Israeli psychologist Ayala Malach Pines. She imagined a kind of 'funnel of love' – her pun, not mine – into which we pour everyone we meet. But just as a funnel gets narrower as it deepens, and lets fewer and fewer elements through, so our criteria naturally get more and more focussed as we eliminate potential partners, until we eventually accept only the ones who really suit. (The criteria we use to create and operate our funnel form the sub-stance of the following chapters of this book.)

What often stops us from using the love fun-nel effectively is a kind of fear of focussing: a nervousness about elimination, a wariness of being choosy, a belief that we shouldn't – for which read 'aren't entitled to' – dismiss partners who mismatch, or partnership options which don't appeal. 'I need to spread the net wide or I won't find anyone' . . . 'If I set the bar too high no one will want me' . . . 'I can't say no to her/him, they'll feel so rejected'. This panic is totally understandable if we've had – as we all have – past heartbreak. But it's nevertheless misguided; we do need to focus on what we want rather than going with the flow. I'm not a believer in 'The One', but unless we start saying no to those who aren't right for us, we won't get anywhere near those who are.

If you suspect that fear of focussing is hold-ing you back, then try this. Imagine yourself sitting somewhere you feel most comfortable, and knowing that your 'right for you' partner is nearby. You're happy because he or she is there, you know that they care for you and you for them and you allow yourself to want them and to want the relationship you have with them. (If you're tempted into caveats or qualifications of the 'nobody loves me' or 'that'll never happen' kind, set these aside for the moment.) Now imagine your partner arrives. Imagine seeing them, hearing their voice as they speak to you, feeling their touch as they reach out for you. Allow yourself to experience their attention fully and know that you deserve that attention.

The point of this exercise is not to imagine what a future partner might actually be like. It's to have a mental experience of wanting that partner, feeling entitled to want them and being wanted in return. As explained at the very start of this book, partner choice is a quest, and as with all quests it's good to have a bit of feisty courage – courage to believe in yourself, courage to believe there are partners out there you can choose, courage to believe that there are partners out there who will choose you. Given that belief, you'll find it much easier to keep setting aside those you don't want and keep heading towards those you do.

Specifying

So how do we begin? How do we create our personal love funnel? The answer is to get more specific. Specificity clears the mind, orders the thinking, makes us feel in control, helps us understand what we're doing. We are right to believe that specifying will help us towards a result, even in an area as unpredictable as partner choice.

The historical wheel has come full circle here. When marriage decisions were made on measurable criteria – age, status, earnings, childbearing potential – specifying was the way to narrow the field. But when romance left its place in the wings and took centre stage, we sniffed at being too precise, because we wanted to let our emotions rule – if we loved each other, surely the details were irrelevant. Now things are coming back into balance. Much of the current coverage of partner choice presents its lessons in the form of specified lists – as seen on every online dating site, in many relationship-advice articles, and via the relationships section on Amazon. The current crop of urban tales featuring heroes/heroines who found their princess/prince through detailed specification

inspires us not only because we too want to mag-
ically conjure up our own fairy-tale partners,
but also because we recognize that specifying is
necessary to the process.

Of course we shouldn't over-specify. It's not
only that, life being what it is, we can't have
everything we want. It's also that many of the
details of what we want will be irrelevant to our
goal of a good relationship. It may matter hugely
that a partner shares our love of animals, but if
they do love animals – or if we fall for them
regardless – it likely won't matter at all that
they have blue eyes rather than brown. Proof of
this is courtesy of another study by Professor
Eli Finkel, in which he asked speed daters their
partner criteria just before the event; said daters then completely ignored their own bench-
marks when they started mingling only minutes
later. However convinced we are that we need a
partner who's extravert/introvert, dark/blonde,
big/small, if we find the right person, size won't
matter.

Even so, once our partner pool is big enough,
specifying is the perfect starting point. It keeps
us on logical track. It boundaries the challenge
and keeps it doable. It engages our minds for a
task which can otherwise all too easily become

over-influenced by our hearts and other more lustful parts of our anatomy. Perhaps unexpectedly, specifying also opens the door to deeper realizations. Nobel Prize winner Daniel Kahneman, whose bestselling book *Thinking, Fast and Slow* recently alerted us to the subtleties of decision-making – or in other words, choice – points out that specifying doesn't just call on logic but also on a more instinctive awareness. He believes that we 'improve . . . intuition by making a list then sleeping on it.' When we create a partner specification, we will often mysteriously find ourselves exploring much wider issues, not just about surface criteria but also about what we need from a partner on a deeper level, and how to instinctively recognize that when it arrives.

Your wish-list

Specifying is the perfect starting point – and the right first step. Our assumption, offline as well as on, is that we should start with what we ourselves are 'selling' and only then consider what we want to 'buy' from a partner. But that's not only the wrong metaphor – partnership is not about trading but about relating – it's also the wrong way round. To attract someone, we first need to know what kind of someone to attract. We can't set the GPS effectively until we know the destination.

If you've already made a wish-list of the specifics you want in a partner, take this opportunity to revisit it. If you haven't already made a list, here's your opportunity. Write down all the elements which for you headline your ideal mate. Gender, age, appearance, cultural background, religious belief, lifestyle, career, earnings, leisure patterns, hobbies, interests, location – if you run out of categories, most online dating sites include an extensive tick-box list. Avoid vague, avoid abstract – the idea is to get a detailed, defined, quantifiable starter guide. Then prioritize in order of importance; as I've said, you can't have everything, so your top five at least need to be the things you couldn't live without.

Deal-breakers

Next, list the things you couldn't live *with*, your deal-breakers. This part of the process aims to make sure we don't find ourselves involved with (worse, married to) someone utterly unsuitable; it's the bottom line which helps us less to find The One – for there are many Ones – as to make sure that The Totally Wrong One doesn't slip under our guard because they are tempting. Here are four classic deal-breakers, and that's about the number to aim for – more, and you're probably drawing the net too tight.

- Different and uncomplementary sexual leanings – such as a potential partner's being gay whereas you need straight, or vice versa
- Mismatched relationship aims – such as their wanting marriage where you want casual, or vice versa
- A conflict in deep values – such as their being highly religious whereas you are allergic to anything remotely spiritual
- Incompatibility of interests – not a gap in enthusiasm, which can often be bridged by encouragement, but a serious mismatch, such as their being a passionate sailor whereas you are aquaphobic

It's tempting not to consider deal-breakers. But we should be clear about what we don't want, especially the elements we are uneasy about not wanting, as they're the ones we may most unwisely give ground on. If we truly couldn't live with someone who has a dangerous job, for example, it's fairer to everyone to be aware of that, rather than denying, compromising, then wobbling.

A 'normal, happy day'

Wish-list made, deal-breakers noted, we next need to specify in a slightly different way. Rather than defining a partner, envision a partnership. What if you woke up one weekday morning five years in the future, having made the perfect choice. Imagine the rest of the day – not special, not peak experience, just normal, solid and satisfying. What might be your plan for this 'normal, happy day'? In what location would you see yourself? What would you do? How would you spend time – with your partner? By yourself? Who else might be there? What sort of lifestyle would you have? How would you feel? Above all, what would be especially rewarding about the relationship you'd created?

This exercise gives new perspective by drawing two crucial distinctions – between dream and actuality and between partner and partnership. Envisioning what we're after not as fantasy but as reality strips away many of the inessentials – things we may hanker after but are irrelevant to our happiness; we may find ourselves altering our wish-lists as a result. Plus the exercise broadens awareness out again, from the partner we might choose to the everyday life we would have with that partner. (This everyday life is, of course, the whole aim of choosing a partner in the first place: I did at one point wonder whether this book should have been called 'How to Choose a Partnership'.) Enhancing detail in this way leaves in place the core needs, but allows us to form a resonant and motivating picture of what we want our future to hold.

Welcoming invitation

How to use these specifications? When doing distance dating, the wish-list and the deal-breakers inform the tick-boxes, while the 'normal, happy day' exercise will give you the material to write the free-text elements of profile and partner specification. There's an added bonus here. Research suggests that, online, it's more compelling – for which read attractive – to structure your profile not as a 'dating CV' (age, interests, holiday plans) but as a welcoming invitation to join you in a relationship; the 'normal, happy day' exercise provides all the essential raw material for such an invitation.

If you're motivated to put in the work, you could also use the material you've gathered to design and apply your own customized matching algorithm. This is precisely what was done by PhD student Chris McKinlay, who apparently had something of a eureka moment when he realized that, rather than relying entirely on personal charisma, he could use his talent as a mathematician to develop a personal formula for a perfect partner. He did so, found love and wrote the bestselling book to prove it. Details of *Optimal Cupid* – and of *Data, a Love Story*, from female counterpart Amy Webb – are in the bibliography.

If partner choice is face-to-face – speed dating, blind dating, meeting with an online suitor

or simple right-place-right-time serendipity –
the wish-list, deal-breakers and 'normal, happy
day' specifications are vital touchstones. With
these kept firmly in mind, we can begin to tally
vision with reality, our desires with flesh and
blood, and start asking ourselves the crucial
questions: Does this person fit our theoretical
specification and, if not, does that matter? We
may well feel it doesn't, if in other ways there is
a fit. Does this person contravene any of our
deal-breakers, and if so, is that contravention
writ in stone? It may well be resolvable with
some negotiation. Finally, but most importantly,
could this person help us create the daily life
that we want for ever? If there's a real possibility they can, that's the best basis for continuing.

6. Connecting

Only connect.

(E. M. Forster, *Howard's End*)

It's surely clear that good relationship decisions are based on knowing far more about a partner than whether they simply tick the headline demands of our wish-list. To return to the 'love funnel' metaphor, the more we filter down our options to fewer possible partners, the more we need to aim for a broader and more extensive understanding of each one.

For there's an addendum to the earlier-mentioned jam experiment. Repeats of the research suggest that the 'shopping mentality' problem is not only down to too much choice but to too little information. Increase our knowledge about each jam (that is, each partner) and choice becomes not only easier but also more accurate, more emotionally intelligent, more successful. So, as we recognize which partners may be right for us, we need to view them from different perspectives, to witness them in different situations, to learn about them and allow them to learn about us – in short, to connect. The slow-river approach again, but this time trawling the deeper waters.

Let's start with the simple fact of meeting. Once upon a time, we knew we were smitten because our eyes met across a crowded room (or at the village well, or as we were tilling the fields). The natural, biologically driven ritual of partner choice is founded on real-life contact.

Yes, some historical courtships were pursued at a distance. Europe in the Middle Ages was awash with ambassadors journeying from royal court to royal court while bearing portraits of beautiful princesses in the hope of arranging advantageous marriages. But without meeting, such long-distance strategies often went horribly wrong: King Henry VIII of England failed to even consummate his marriage to fourth wife Anne of Cleves because when she arrived for the wedding, he realized that 'she is nothing as fair as she hath been reported'.

To really connect with – and make a decision on – a partner, we need to see, to hear, to literally feel them. It was anthropologist David Givens who in 1978 mapped out for us the instinctive process of natural attraction. We glimpse a potential partner from afar, then engage by eye contact, then by talking, then touch, eventually getting close enough to smell, taste and, if the stars align, be sexual. At each stage we parallel our conscious appraisal by unconsciously rating the other's physical appearance, the way they move and speak, their hormonal invitations. At this early stage, closer and closer contact filters partners, not only because of what they say and do, but also because of the way they say it and do it. (Those who make the cut are likely not only to attract us but to be attracted to us; if face-to-face connection leads to a 'yes', it's likely to become a virtuous, circular reinforcing 'yes'.)

Twenty-three days

Actually, we know all this. We intuitively trust face-to-face contact because we realize it gives us essential knowledge on which to base judgement. We are reluctant to develop a relationship before meeting someone, because we know that without face-to-face contact we can't make a full assessment. Which is why when it comes to the distance dating of new technology we may be fascinated but we're also wary; traditional partner choice follows a 'meet-look-talk-touch' model, while new technology follows the new pattern of 'view-read-write-talk-meet-touch', which leaves the really important bit to almost the very end.

Question: How can that work? Answer: It often doesn't. We may find that, after crashing the internet with reciprocally enthusiastic emails for several weeks, when we finally get close to our online crush it's loathing at first sight. Moreover, studies suggest that disappointment when face-to-face rises in direct proportion to how long we've been in other sorts of contact before meeting. In other words, whether our expectations are met depends almost entirely on how long we've been stacking up those expectations. The key number here, according to a recent study at the University of South Florida, is twenty-three days of email; after that, a suitor would have to be a deity-come-to-earth in order to measure up face-to-face.

It's no coincidence that the site- and app-developers, having made their mark promoting a form of dating that was literally at a distance, are currently putting huge effort and budget into trying to reduce that distance and replicate the natural first step of crowded-room eye-catching. The current direction is not just for increased accessibility through profile pictures, audio and video, but for meet-ups, social evenings, dance classes and singles holidays, as well as apps that reveal which of those sitting in the same coffee bar are looking for love tonight. The litmus test will always be the 'close enough to smell' connection.

Distance benefits

That said, we're wrong to be wholly wary of distance in a dating medium. For when it comes to thoughts and feelings, being apart can actually be more trustworthy and more revelatory. A study from Cornell University suggests we're more likely to tell the truth in an email than in a voice conversation, because we know our words are literally down in black and white and can be checked. We're also more likely to open up about significant thoughts and feelings online than face-to-face, because being less close to a prospective partner lowers the fear of rejection and leaves us more able to be authentic. The adrenalin rush that comes with the ping of 'you've got mail' stems not just from the potential of a new relationship but from the fact that the mail in question may contain deep emotional revelations – and the fact that we can respond in kind.

So here's how to drive distance dating to best effect. Benefit from the larger numbers to spot possible candidates, but rather than staying with 'winks' or 'likes', move to email as quickly as possible. Then, at that email level, without getting over-demanding, dive below surface chat; ask serious questions, give serious answers, open up and let partners do the same. The deeper revelations will help gauge the deeper compatibility; if it's there, move on to phoning and meeting – the gold standard of real life.

Proximity and chemistry

For contact makes everything tangible, not only physically but also emotionally. It adds in all the wonderful elements which circumvent our logical brain – there's a reason why Eros is shown with an arrow of love which pierces straight to the heart. It's almost a cliché, that total fixation of gaze and suspension of logical thought. Think Maria and Tony in *West Side Story*, stepping across the dance floor to touch each other. Think

Marius and Cosette in *Les Misérables*, stopping in their tracks at the Luxembourg Gardens as their eyes meet for the first time.

This isn't, contrary to what we might think, only about desire. It's also that simple proximity matters hugely and biases hugely. Once there's a basic attraction, the more time we spend close to someone, the more they will seem appealing, lovable, simply better. And the longer, more frequently, more regularly we spend time with them, the deeper the impact. A 1930s study of 5,000 American couples showed that 45 per cent of them had got together when living within a few blocks of each other, which – while not as surprising in the 1930s as it would be nowadays – is still remarkable.

A word here about 'chemistry', a factor so prized and persuasive that an entire online dating site is named after it. We've surely all experienced the sort of heartfelt mutual liking which leaves us feeling good about ourselves as well as about the other person. But it's difficult to pin down – and research hasn't shown – what exactly chemistry is, let alone what causes it. Basic biological urge? Complex psychological fit? And should we factor it into our choice strategy? Without chemistry most of us would hesitate to

West Side Story. Love at first sight with score by Leonard Bernstein, words by Stephen Sondheim and choreography by Jerome Robbins.

take things further with a partner, and many
commentators feel its absence is a deal-breaker;
the founder of eHarmony, Neil Clark Warren,
states uncompromisingly that unless you feel
the urge to kiss a prospective partner by the
third date 'you're probably never going to feel it'.
But other dating experts join with many traditional cultures in judging chemistry as no
predictor of partnership success; perhaps the
only thing that chemistry guarantees is chemistry. If so, then maybe instead of demanding it as
a prerequisite for a relationship, we ought to be
seeing it as a distracting delusion.

Decision-making strategies

Which is why – unromantic though it may
seem – it's good to add in some more measurable, more strategic, less instinctive criteria for
judging. It's a wise exercise, as first meeting
evolves into regular contact, to ask yourself
what evidence you use as you form your opin-
ion. (It may help to consider here how you judge
not only partners, but anyone close – friends,
colleagues, even family.)

Do you reach conclusions about a person because of . . .

> . . . how they look?
> . . . what they say?
> . . . what they actually do in practice as
> opposed to what they say?
> . . . what their general reputation is?
> . . . what the important people in your life
> think about them?
> . . . how you feel emotionally when you
> are with them?
> . . . how you feel emotionally when they
> are not there but you are thinking
> about them?
> . . . your sexual contact, if any?
> . . . what their friends and family are
> like?
> . . . how they interact with their friends,
> family, colleagues?
> . . . how they interact with your friends,
> family, colleagues?
> . . . their previous life in general?
> . . . their relationship track-record in par-
> ticular?
> . . . what your gut reaction tells you?

Try dividing the elements into those you would always check, and those you'd never bother with because they seem unlinked, irrelevant, impossible to judge. Next, put the list in chronological order, according to those checks you pay attention to first, those you usually leave for later, and those you never attend to. Are there any surprises there?

Then think back. How has this decision-making strategy of yours actually played out? If less than perfectly, how could you improve? Perhaps you could prioritize the elements that until now you've left until later. Perhaps you could place less reliance on some kinds of evidence and more on others. Perhaps you need to extend, to use a wider range of checks and balances so your decision-making's more effective.

An interesting thought about initial moments: one of my early psychology tutors suggested that the first experience we have of a partner provides a snapshot of our entire future relationship, sets the scene, writes the script for later plot development. So, if in their initial meeting Mary finds herself listening to Tom hammer on about his ex, she could find that Tom's past dominates their future relationship. If in their initial meeting Tom and Mary find themselves agreeing easily about where to go to eat, they're likely to have a cooperative time ahead.

So have there been any first meetings that, in hindsight, should have told you to turn and flee? Have there been any first meetings that, in hindsight, you should have taken as the starting point for something important? No regrets – the past is over – but maybe such meetings can be a touchstone as you go forward.

Three elements

If face-to-face compatibility's confirmed and what we want is a simple liaison, we need demand very little more than passion and opportunity. If we are seeking something deeper, the criteria are more complex; below the intensity and the delight, there's a need for a deeper compatibility. As Joanne Woodward apparently said of her five-decade marriage to Paul Newman, 'Sexiness wears thin after a while and beauty fades. But to be married to a man who makes you laugh every day . . . that's a real treat.' So, can we get – can we give – that kind of treat, whether through laughter or otherwise, with our partner?

He wondered how long it would take his partner to join him at the summit, given that they'd set off in different directions to begin with.

If we can, we're likely looking at connection across three elements: values, life goals and personality traits:

- *Values:* what makes our existence most worthwhile: safety, excitement, social recognition, happiness, self-respect, status.
- *Life goals:* the achievements we crave during a lifetime: career success, financial security, travel, adventure, marriage, children.
- *Personality:* a combination of character and temperament: honesty, mental acuity, kindness, generosity, bravery, commitment to hard work.

There's a numbers problem here. I've just enumerated a longish list of examples to cover all three elements, but I could have devoted an entire chapter (or indeed a whole book) to each. For, while a full tally of a partner's hobbies is typically achievable on the fingers of one hand, the possible subcategories of these three deeper levels might number more than the hairs on one's head. Far too many elements to keep count of, let alone keep in mind as a benchmark for partner choice. Better to explore these issues more broadly to reveal what's really important.

Three questions

The next exercise lets you attempt this broader exploration. It has as its starting point a somewhat morbid topic, but it's useful to help you reflect. Imagine you are on your deathbed. You are looking back on a good life. You've experienced what you were meant to experience, done what you were meant to do, are ending as you are meant to end. Now ask yourself these questions:

1. What three values made your life most worthwhile? (Think benefits such as safety, happiness, etc.)
2. Which three goals have you achieved in your life that you are most satisfied with and proud of? (Think aims such as career success, adventure, etc.)
3. What three personality traits do you most want other people to praise you for when you have gone? (Think descriptors such as honesty, generosity, etc.)

Answer these three questions, get your nine answers, and you'll have a top-line list of what is deeply important in your life and thus what needs to be deeply important to your partner in his or her life. If one of your key values is status, you'll want a partner to rate that too. If your dream is to parent an entire football team of offspring, your ideal partner will be one who shares that goal – forgive the pun. If it matters to you to work hard, you'll need a partner willing to pull all-nighters alongside you, or at the least give you a genuinely appreciative hug when you finally come to bed at 6 a.m.

Proofs of love

Nine words are a great start, a good snapshot. Problem is, almost always we'll choose words that – while meaningful – are also abstract, indefinite, lacking detail. Example: almost everyone who does this exercise mentions the word 'love'. But what particular flavour of love is that – and what if it's not to a prospective partner's taste? What if our idea of 'love' consists of huge amounts of free time apart, and theirs is 24/7

gazing into each other's eyes? What if we agree
with St Paul that 'love is patient, love is kind',
while our partner is more of the Woody Allen
school of thought that says 'love is suffering'.

Fanfares please for counsellor Gary Chapman's bestselling book *The Five Love Languages*,
which makes just this point. He suggests we
each have our own vocabulary of ways we feel
cared for, as does our beloved – but discrepancy
between our respective visions creates relationship booby traps. Chapman's list of five languages is as follows: words of affirmation, quality
time, receiving gifts, acts of service, physical
touch – though there are surely more one could
creatively add to the list. And it's pretty clear
where the traps might lie. If our partner's top
love-language is gifts and ours is words of affirmation, then however many delightful presents
they bring home, we'll still feel unappreciated if
they don't say those three little words. If our top
criterion is quality time spent together, while
our partner defines love as acts of service, then
however many romantic weekends we surprise
them with, they won't be satisfied if we don't occasionally take the rubbish out.

What are your proofs of love? Define them
as concretely as you can. Then list just as con-

cretely the 'proofs' of all your deathbed answers. What do you mean by 'safety' – is that financial, practical or emotional? What are you thinking of when you talk about 'career success' – promotion, work satisfaction or appreciation from your team? What do you have in mind when you talk of 'generosity' – is that giving of your time, your money, your energy? Think through these deeper meanings so that, when the time's right, you can explain them to a partner and teach them how to be good for you.

Sameness

It's clear that we need a partner to accept, appreciate and approve of these elements of us. But do we need them to copy, to match exactly, to be a 'bird of a feather' that 'flock[s] together'? Here we call on the insights of psychiatrist Hellmuth Kaiser, who in the 1940s, while watching identical twins ice-skate in perfect harmony, suddenly realized that the audience's rapt fascination was due more to the synchronicity of the siblings than to their technical skill. We human beings like sameness. It makes us feel secure; babies even a few minutes old gurgle with glee when adults mirror their movements. It makes us feel validated; imitation is flattering, so strengthens our good feeling about ourselves.

This good feeling's reciprocal, a virtuous circle; if we worship a partner because we're alike, they'll probably worship us back. Which is why most dating systems, from online to matchmaking, pair clients based on likeness. And certainly when it comes to values and life goals, this approach is quite correct. Pair with someone who's taking the same track in life and we'll be content; if we're on opposite tracks we'll either move apart at speed, or play tug-of-war. Love, as Antoine de Saint-Exupéry famously wrote, consists 'not in two people looking at each other, but two people looking outwards in the same direction'.

With personality it's slightly more complicated, the research is more contradictory and it's possible opposites really do attract. Yes, same-personality partners may make good buddies. But there may not be enough spark for interest, let alone romance, not enough complementarity for day-to-day teamwork, let alone home-building, child-rearing and balancing all the spinning plates of a practical life together. As an example, in *Little Women*, Louisa May Alcott's novel about girls growing up in Civil War

America, Jo March makes a fast friend of Laurie, the boy next door. Their bond is close and strong, but when Laurie falls in love with Jo, she is sensible enough to realize that their similarly masculine attitudes and hot-tempered personalities mean they could never make a good match. Instead, she moves to New York and there meets academic Friedrich Bhaer, whose tender character complements rather than copies her own; under his guidance she fulfils her potential, while Laurie ends up equally happily married to more feminine, less tempestuous Amy March. The lesson Alcott offers us – and one which relationship-advice books have repeated down the ages – is that we should choose a mate with similar values and goals, but with a different personality.

That said, recent research from the University of Columbia suggests it's more complex than that. Apparently a better answer is to ask a further question: What do individuals want? Those of us who feel good around similarity will thrive with a partner as like us as possible. Those of us energized around difference will thrive with a dissimilar mate. It's not the dynamic itself – all variations can theoretically work – it's our comfort level that dictates success.

What about the 'men are from Mars, women are from Venus' issue? We might wonder whether, if similarity is so very important, but X and Y chromosomes are so irreversibly unlike, all different-gender relationships are going to be fraught. Here's the reassurance: men and women are actually very similar. Some psychologists even suggest there are only two built-in gender differences – verbal skill and aggression – while anything else is down to nurture not nature and therefore adaptable. So if a relationship ends unhappily we shouldn't blame the gender difference, or point accusingly at 'men' or 'women'. And if a relationship seems well advised, we shouldn't worry that it's all doomed just because our beloved is of a particular gender. To put it another way: 'Men are from earth, women are from earth. Deal with it.' (The original of that quote is claimed by at least a dozen people, but it was far too apposite to omit from this book just because its author can't be identified!)

Disrobing

Values, life goals, personality. Given honest conversation, we can probably guestimate these

'Commitment is an act, not a word.' – Jean-Paul Sartre

three elements in the first few meetings with a potential partner and – as we should – bail out if there are reasons for doubt . . .

But real proof at this level takes a while, and it's as important to talk as it is to listen. Revealing what matters to us, doing the things that fascinate us, exploring the past and planning the future together will over time remove more and more individual 'veils', and, along with that disrobing, our judgement of each other will become more and more accurate. Studies suggest that goals will become obvious first, values next, with personality revealed last of all. To slightly hasten the process, you might try raising the 'deathbed questions' as a topic for mutual discussion; crassly posed, they may bring the conversation to a shuddering halt, but used at a stage where both partners are sufficiently at ease to go deeper, they're exceedingly good for highlighting compatibilities.

Embroidery

Speaking of veils, is it wise to 'embroider' them in the early going, perhaps omitting certain details and subtly altering others for effect? How should we present ourselves in order to attract a mate? Answer: don't 'present', simply be. Of course it's tempting to massage the headline figures – online, apparently women often lower their age and weight, while men increase their height and salary. And of course it's courteous not to be so 'open and honest' that we spend the first few dates revealing intimate details of our most recent relationship-breakdown or the exact figures of our current financial crisis. But if we're not at least factually truthful to begin with, and if we're not emotionally truthful very soon after, we're in grave danger of ending up with a partner who wants what we say we are, not what we actually are.

Which is why I'm no fan of dating systems such as *The Rules*, which advise a 'play hard-to-get' approach to partner choice. I have to admit to feeling faintly nauseated by a book which, as early as line nineteen of its introduction, promises a way of acting around a guy so he becomes 'obsessed with you and wants to commit' – surely patronizing to both genders. But my objections are not only ideological but also pragmatic – any suitor, male or female, who is only enthralled by the thrill of the 'hard-to-get' chase will likely lose interest once the hunt is over. Although being authentic may feel scary, the more authentic we can be – about what we believe, what we want, who we are – the more chance we'll have of eventually meeting a suitable prince or princess, even if that also means that en route we drive off a lot of incompatible frogs.

What if, conversely, we wonder if a partner is being inauthentic? This isn't so much about whether they are lying – if we suspect they are, we're almost certainly right. But what if nerves are holding them back, or lack of self-confidence is making them hide true thoughts and feelings. Usually only time, trust and the opportunity for in-depth conversation will tell. But – though it isn't under our control and shouldn't be magicked up to order – an external drama or crisis will often make it clear, snapping us out of early courtship timidity, giving us a reason to step out and show who we really are, for bad or for good.

I am remembering one client whose turning point for leaving a boyfriend was when she was involved in an accident and he suggested she call a cab to take her to A & E as he was 'too tired' to drive her there. More hopefully for one's faith in human nature, I'm remembering another client who suffered a burglary; her partner's absolute support, practical action and complete understanding of how traumatized she was sent her rightly over the edge into commitment. It was sad about the burglary, but for the relationship, it was a result.

Soothe then solve

The two stories above, highlighting two very different responses to the emotional needs of a partner, bring us neatly to another kind of connection. And if you're reading this book in the hope of a single 'top tip', here it comes. Without this element in a relationship, all the compatibility in the world won't keep us afloat; with it, all the alarms, excursions, dramas and crises won't sink us. Professor Sue Johnson, on whose work this section of the book is based, even hints that every other single factor involved in partner choice may be irrelevant. Get this right and you're sorted.

I'm talking about emotional responsiveness – a partner's ability to pay loving attention to our emotional needs, and our ability to pay attention to theirs. Note the reciprocity. As well as needing to choose a partner who values our feelings, we need to choose a partner who motivates us to value theirs. However wonderful a suitor, if they don't inspire us to respond, they're the wrong choice.

We all have emotional needs. Abraham Maslow's famous hierarchy of needs – that triangle at whose base sit the human physical requirements for air, water, food, clothing, shelter and safety – has on its higher storeys the need for belonging, acceptance, security, respect, love. We generate much of this inside ourselves as we mature, but the meaning of John Donne's cry that 'no man is an island' is that none of us can do the job alone. Knowing our partner will respond when we need them, knowing we'll respond when they need us, is at the heart of the love bond.

So what is this responsiveness? Here's a definition which you may find useful:

1. Being able to notice, pay attention to, reflect on, soothe and express our own emotions.
2. Being able to notice, pay attention to, reflect on, soothe and respond to a partner's emotions.
3. Being able to reflect on and discuss the interaction between 1 and 2.

4. Being able to do all the above even when a partner can't, won't or doesn't want to.

Notice what's missing: any mention of solutions. Solutions may be vital, but a partner's unlikely to even hear them, let alone do anything with them, until emotions are being honoured. So first soothe. Only then, solve.

At home by the fire

Let's look at this another way, not as a list but a story. One of my favourite books is Thomas Hardy's *Far from the Madding Crowd* – where headstrong Bathsheba Everdene turns down a proposal from good-hearted employee Gabriel Oak. Instead she marries dashing Sergeant Troy and, when he abandons her, accepts the courtship of reserved neighbour William Boldwood. Just to be clear, while there's tragedy, there are no absolute villains in this story. In their own way, everyone does their best.

But only one man – Oak – is worthy of Bathsheba. That's not just because he supports her practically through his work on the farm, but also because he is the only one who can stand firm emotionally. Sergeant Troy's passion seduces Bathsheba but his feelings are unreliable, while Boldwood is emotionally crippled. Only Oak is capable of empathic generosity; in Hardy's words, 'the [things] which affected Gabriel's personal well-being were not the most absorbing and important in his eyes'. If you've read the novel, you'll know the ending. If not, then take a clue from Gabriel's proposal to Bathsheba – which at first she rejects as uninspiring, but later learns to treasure: 'at home by the fire, whenever you look up there I shall be – and whenever I look up, there will be you.'

Emotional engagement

Which makes it all sound very simple. But this kind of maturity is a big ask. It means, as Gabriel Oak knows, being there for a partner over time and under all circumstances. It means staying calm even when sad, angry or anxious. It means staying engaged even when our partner is sad, angry or anxious and we are sorely tempted to tell them to get a grip. It means staying rock-solid even when our partner is firing negative emotions, with us as the target – as they will do from time to time in even the most loving relationship. Easy? Not at all.

So are we warranted in making emotional responsiveness a benchmark for partner choice? So long as we give back, surely it's entirely reasonable to expect a potential partner to deliver emotional support, entirely justifiable to walk away if they can't or won't. Science is on my side in this. A landmark fourteen-year study by Professor Ted Huston of the University of Texas at Austin suggests that where partners aren't emotionally concerned about each other during courtship, then even if they decide to wed they'll probably part in the end. If couples are consistently kind, warm, sympathetic and empathic from the start, they're hugely more likely to stay the course. We not only can, but should, make emotional responsiveness a relationship deal-breaker.

You may at this point be wondering about the widespread belief that such demands could never be made of those with the Y chromosome. So can men respond emotionally? The answer is absolutely yes. Any male wariness of emotion is not because men feel it less – physiologically they actually experience it more strongly, more painfully, hence the wariness. Men's main

Adam realized at once that this relationship was going to be
emotionally demanding.

handicap is conditioning; little boys are told not to cry, big boys are told to 'be a man', but what they're rarely told is how to manage their emotions. But another study from the University of Texas suggests that when told empathy is attractive and that emotional responsiveness makes for good relationships, men are totally capable of stepping up. I know this first-hand. I have had as clients many men who fully take on board this particular relationship challenge, reach out to their partners and respond to their partners reaching out to them. These men are certainly brave – but they're not unique. There are lots of them out there.

Proofs of responsiveness

Earlier in this chapter, we needed to get very specific about values, goals and personality – thinking through what our definitions were, deciding what 'proof' there might be that we can deliver what a partner might need and vice versa. In the same way, it's good to get specific about emotional responsiveness – what we mean by it, how we would know it if we saw it – or we again risk a relationship minefield where what one partner wants is not what the other can give.

How to unearth your definition? One good way is to think of the last time you actively felt emotionally supported; what did people say and do (or not say and do) to bring you back into balance? As contrast, when did you last feel unsupported; what went on that left you disappointed and discouraged? What were the differences between those times that made such a difference in how you felt?

Can we tell if a potential partner is capable of responding? It's unwise to even try to judge this in the early going, when heavy-duty emotional interaction is rarely appropriate, let alone needed. That said, the following are excellent signs, their absence worrying: if a suitor listens with concentration when we are speaking, reveals emotional awareness when they are speaking, and – a sneaky one, this – shows empathy to those in the vicinity, even though these people are clearly not the object of courtship attention. One of my friends married a woman who on their first date behaved well to a waiter when he accidentally spilled soup in her lap. Another friend instantly dumped a beau who was rude to a nervous server. On both occasions my verdict was: good choice.

Serious tests of this dimension will likely come when strong and uncomfortable emotions first bite – on occasions that might be as huge as a bereavement or as small as a hellish commute from work. A partner may be able to listen, comfort, sympathize and soothe – and we may accept that from them, or not. We may be able to listen, comfort, sympathize and soothe – and a partner may let us in, or not. We need to pay close attention, for it's here that both sides will show their true colours. And it's here we will find the answers to the two questions which Sue Johnson claims are most crucial to relationship success: 'Can I be there for you? Can you be there for me?'

Paul and Linda

What if the answer to the first question – can I be there for you? – is actually 'no'? If we don't feel inspired to deliver emotionally to a partner, we need to ask ourselves why and then listen carefully to whatever reasons our minds and hearts give back. 'Because I'm just not motivated enough with this person' is extremely useful information, even though it probably signals an ending.

The answer to the second question – can you be there for me? – may be unclear. We may sense a partner's willingness but the way they respond to our 'bids' for care may not be quite what we need – a loss of attention, a turn away, an unresponsive comment. Is this just cause for dismissal? If all other signs are good it's surely unfair to call a halt without giving a partner at least a chance to step up. So perhaps we ask, clearly and without criticism, for the response we need when we're emotional? Listening or cuddling. Asking questions or staying silent. Looking on the bright side or joining in the pessimism. Giving time alone or being willing to stay for a while. While we're on the subject, we might even turn the conversation to asking what response a partner might need from us when they are distressed. Just so we know.

This depth of conversation may not be possible at once. And those few preceding paragraphs may seem more like advice on how to relate to a partner than advice on how to choose one. But a huge element of successful decision-making is finding out whether each partner is both able and motivated to actually learn what the other person needs and what the relationship may demand. If either of us can't or won't learn then, harsh as it may sound, there is no future. If we're prepared to study, the future is shining bright.

Apparently when Paul McCartney and his first wife, Linda, married, they made a private vow: 'I will never put you down'. To my mind, this didn't only mean that they would never insult or disparage each other. It didn't only mean that they would never betray or abandon each other. It meant that they would never stop being aware of each other's feelings, never stop giving attention to each other's needs, never fail to open up to each other, never fail to reply. Emotional responsiveness at its best.

Four tendencies

We come now to perhaps the most intricate of all issues by which we may assess relationship potential – how we relate, not just when one of us has an emotional need but when the connection between us threatens to fray.

Because all of us will inevitably, at some

point in our relationship, feel insecure, even unloved. Where we differ is what we do with that.
At the heart of understanding what we need in
a partner is understanding just how we differ,
and how that plays out.

For which insight, we thank psychologists
John Bowlby and Mary Ainsworth and their
work on child development (which, for easier
consumption, I've here simplified). Bowlby
began, in the mid years of the twentieth century,
with a simple but innovative idea: that for humans, life is insecure. This starts early. We lose
trust when we are propelled at birth into a world
that is totally unlike the safe and comforting
womb we just left. We lose more trust when,
however devoted our carers, they're sometimes
too distracted, busy or stressed to give us the attention we need. Yes, we survive, and largely
we survive well. But underneath it all we're still
mistrustful, fearing that we won't be loved and
if we are that love will disappear – when such
insecurity hits, we fall back on our own individual coping mechanisms, 'attachment' tendencies, as Bowlby called them.

Mary Ainsworth built on this theory with an
in-depth study of seventy-six toddlers and their
mothers, exploring more fully what these coping

mechanisms might be. Mum and baby were shown into a room full of toys and with a research assistant on hand. Once toddler was happily playing, Mum left the room three times for three-minute intervals – during the last time the research assistant also left. Some little ones cried at first, then calmed, seeming 'secure' that Mum would come back. Some became 'anxious', and when Mum returned, clung on in case she went away again. Yet others protested by cutting off, ignoring Mum on her return, punishing her for her absence; Ainsworth called this 'avoidant' behaviour. Others got angry with Mum for leaving; I'm naming this tendency 'attacking'. Four toddler reactions, four emotional strategies, four tendencies to behave a particular way when feeling insecure, unloved and wary that love might never return.

As adults . . .

A few decades on from Bowlby and Ainsworth's work and we see a growing realization that these tendencies don't just fade as a child grows up. As adults, we're certainly more secure because we're more in control of our world, but we also repeatedly learn – often through the route of heart-break – that we can't always trust that world to deliver. And we still harbour those four attach-ment tendencies, sometimes majoring in one, mostly doing mix-and-match to differing de-grees. When we are 'secure', trusting in ourselves and others, we handle love situations with calm-ness and confidence – even if in the end a rela-tionship dies. When 'anxious' we are worried by love, unsure of our competence and needing re-assurance. As 'avoidant', we fight shy of emo-tional engagement, pull away if commitment looms. 'Attacking', we feel an inner frustration, perhaps creating conflict in order to connect.

If any of this sounds familiar, you're right. We all have all these tendencies in different proportions. We may not manifest the more challenging ones except when we feel insecure or feel a relationship connection weakening – but they're there in all of us. For that, no blame, no shame; attachment tendencies are the human condition.

Which of course is why so many characters in literature and film display them (aside, of course, from the 'secure' tendency, which is so mature and wise that it has zero dramatic po-tential). The other tendencies, however, provide endless raw material for compulsive characters and angst-driven plot. For 'anxious', see Bridget Jones's romantic insecurity and her readiness to cling again and again to Daniel Cleaver even when he behaves badly (though thankfully, in the end, she sees the light and walks away). As an example of 'avoidant', we might turn to the butler Stevens who, in Kazuo Ishiguro's novel *The Remains of the Day*, is so wary of the relationship that might develop if he showed his true feelings for housekeeper Miss Kenton that he fails to admit his love over a period of several decades. For 'attacking', we need look no further than Heathcliff and Catherine in Emily Brontë's novel *Wuthering Heights*; while they think of themselves as one – 'Whatever souls are made of, his and mine are the same' – they are nevertheless endlessly intense with each other and Heathcliff in particular can often only express his love for Catherine through absolute rage.

These tendencies have had an undeserved bad press. As is clear from the last paragraph, particularly when they're presented in art rather than real life, they're often seen as being all downside, fault and weakness. 'Secure' is, rightly, viewed as the poster child for happy and mature relationships. But the other tendencies have their upsides too. Being anxious may mean we're motivated to ride out a partnership storm, stay loyal, stay committed. Being avoidant may mean a certain emotional independence, the ability to give partners space. An attacking tendency can mean being comfortable with dissension, or being able to summon huge intensity and passion.

So, to what extent do you stay calm and serene, trusting in life and love to give you what you need? How far do you stay loyal – even though you also sometimes cling? How far do you maintain your emotional independence – albeit you may get accused of not caring? How far do you engage energetically – granted that you occasionally pick fights? How do you respond when you feel love sliding away from you? What, in short, are you going to bring to the partnership table when you feel less than fully connected?

Partner tendencies

And what will a partner bring to the table? Discovering that is never going to be as simple as gauging height and weight, values and life goals, or a capacity for emotional responsiveness. Crucially, attachment tendencies may not kick in at the start of a relationship because at that point we likely feel perfectly loved and perfectly secure. So how can we make at least a top-level guess on a beloved's tendencies in time to make a reasoned decision?

Here's a useful diagnostic. Sex. Sex is one of the arenas where a person is most themselves, and reveals that self most early and openly in a relationship. It is Sue Johnson who here again offers guidance. She suggests that sex which involves a healthy balance between physical pleasure and emotional bonding might be called 'synchrony sex' and reflects a secure tendency. Sex used largely for comfort and as a way to calm doubts or conflicts, which Johnson terms 'solace sex', suggests a tendency to be anxious. Sex that is self-focussed, performance-oriented, with little emotional openness, could be labelled 'sealed off' sex; it signals avoidant tendencies. I would add that energetic, forceful, 'fight it all out' passion is what one might call 'squabble sex' and might reflect an attacking tendency.

Again, these are tendencies, not types. All of us make love in all the above styles – with emotion, for reassurance, as self-gratification, to let out frustration – in fact my guess is that if you mixed all four together what you'd get would be sex labelled 'normal'. But a noticeable preponderance of one type or the other can act as a Rorschach test, revealing who a potential partner is and what a potential partnership with them might be like.

Tom and Jerry

What do attachment tendencies suggest for partner choice? Similarity can work. When both of us are anxious or attacking we'll understand each other and thrive on our mutual need for security or strong engagement. When we're both avoidant – that is, if we ever manage to get together in the first place – we may feel constant gratitude for the reciprocal freedom.

Dissimilarity can play well too. If we compensate for each other, some anxious dependency may strengthen the bond; a small amount of avoidant independence may stabilize interactions; a little attacking engagement may mean issues get put on the table and dealt with in healthy short order. (A good exercise, at this point, is not only to remember your own past relationships but also look at the ones you see around you, as acted out by friends, family or colleagues. Playing 'spot the attachment tendency' is not only good practice for understanding partners-to-be but also good fun.)

But do be wary of extremes. If we meet a partner who pushes for commitment on the first date, one who's never had any relationships longer than a few weeks, or one who picks a fight within minutes of meeting, beware. We are facing respectively an off-the-scale anxious, off-the-scale avoidant and off-the-scale attacking personality. Unless we're totally convinced we can handle it, we shouldn't even try.

The more subtle, and often less easily spottable, combination from hell is when partners of different tendencies date but can't accommodate. Initial attraction may be strong – contrast makes for interest – and when we're safely in love there may be no trigger for attachment wobbles. But fast forward a little: inject any kind of stress or insecurity and the dynamic will make both sides crazy. Anxious plus avoidant means one of us clings, the other pulls away. Avoidant plus attacking means one of us runs, the other pushes to engage. Attacking plus anxious means one fights, the other fears. The result can be a Tom and Jerry cartoon-type chase, with A emotionally pursuing B round the room of the relationship. If you've ten years of commitment behind you by the time this sort of thing creeps in, it's absolutely worth taking time, energy and counselling to resolve it. But if it's happening a mere ten days or weeks into a new relationship, run for your life.

The ideal

The ideal here – and it is an ideal – is that mostly we are secure with each other and that at least one of us is secure most of the time. Yes, there'll be bouts of wobble – but in terms of choosing a partner, what to look for is someone largely honest and direct, who communicates clearly and is not into game-playing. Someone who is aware of emotion, not afraid of intimacy and is open to the possibility of commitment. In other words, human, but largely sorted.

But there's a problem. What I've just described can easily be experienced not as ideal but as boring. Remove the emotional roller-coaster tendencies of anxiety, avoidance and attack, and what's left can feel all too calm. It's easy to get confused and think that because someone isn't any kind of a problem, they are no kind of a partner. I have had clients who in the same breath as describing their relationship as 'the most secure I've had', express doubts that it is 'the real thing'; clients who, while reporting contentment, worry that what they're experiencing is too effortless to be true love.

In fact, secure is good, contented is something to be glad about, and the occasional tempest is exhilarating but constant storms are exhausting. If in the past we have experienced a feeling of secure contentment with a partner but didn't choose them, that was our loss. And if in the future we experience that kind of security in a relationship, then – assuming all other boxes are ticked – we should offer up heartfelt thanks and hang on for dear life.

7. Being in Love

Anthony Carthew: 'And [you are], I suppose, in love?'
Lady Diana Spencer: 'Of course!'
Charles, Prince of Wales: 'Whatever "in love" means.'

(ITN interview on the engagement
of Charles and Diana, *1981*)

I am a huge believer not only in the possibility but also the wisdom of falling in love. It's a magical, sparkly feeling. The world seems bright and shiny, the future seems glorious, everything seems possible. Yes, being in love can sometimes be hard – as the classic French ballad has it, 'the pleasure of love lasts a moment, the pain of love lasts a lifetime.' But the excitement, the arousal and the adoration are surely irresistible. Everyone should be love-struck at least once in their life.

Two examples. In Charles Dickens's novel, the eponymous David Copperfield first meets Dora Spenlow when he visits her father's house. 'All was over . . . I was gone, headlong.' There follows a delightful description of the ecstasy that comes with having 'fulfilled my destiny . . . in an abyss of love'.

And in case we think that fiction always exaggerates reality, let us also recall footballer David Beckham's equal wonderment at first seeing Victoria on a Spice Girls video: 'I thought "she is . . . perfection".' Their later face-to-face meeting, at a charity football match, happily led to David's infatuation being fully returned and an almost instant relationship, engagement and marriage.

Fixation

But what does being 'in love' have to do with effective relationship choice? In some ways, not a lot. In evolutionary terms, this rush of wonderful emotion was originally designed not to help us choose a compatible match, but to help us stand by a partner with whom we were making babies. Lust was there to get us rolling in the hay, being 'in love' was there to make us willing to push the pram alongside the one we'd originally sneaked off to the barn with. The 'in love' flurry of the hormones known as 'mono-amines' exists to focus us on partnership through those early years when offspring need us to stay close, to the exclusion of all else. So much so that research at the University of Pisa has found key similarities between the mono-amine levels of new partners and those who suffer obsessive-compulsive disorder. When we fall for someone we become literally fixated on them – as David Copperfield describes it, 'a captive and a slave'.

There's a less evolutionary, more psycholog-ical and – in this age of family planning – less offspring-focussed set of reasons why 'in love' is so compelling. It's that when we fall in love, we're following an emotional dream of being the centre of the world. While very small, unless our childhood was damaged, those around us did their best to keep us absolutely safe, warm, cared for, loved. We leave that behind as we grow to adulthood, but we'll always be looking for it again, always be wanting to recreate the secu-rity and the validation that was ours in the early years. 'In love' holds out the promise that our beloved will make us the centre of their world, and for ever. No wonder it's an obsessive com-pulsion.

We build on that compulsion. When in love, we're likely to spend huge amounts of time together – proximity, you may remember, strengthens attraction. We stay close, connecting through sex but also through matched body language, emotional revelation and deep eye contact. The effectiveness of those last two elements was fascinatingly demonstrated by psychologist Arthur Aron, who got previously unintroduced subjects falling head over heels with each other simply by having them ask each other a series of thirty-six self-disclosure questions, then gazing into one another's eyes for a mere four minutes. This approach was later used in an experiment to raise the 'take-up factor' for speed daters – and indeed those daters who asked more personal questions and gave more revealing answers got more picks from the evening.

The wrong roller coaster?

The problem is that thereafter we may get stuck. For though I hate to be the bearer of bad news, none of that wonderful falling-in-love experience is guaranteed to produce long-term compatibility. Literature is riddled with stories of how initial adoration translates badly into

It's best to choose a roller-coaster ride that brings you back down to earth both safely and without nausea.

ordinary everyday life: Anna Karenina and Count Vronsky; Madame Bovary and Rodolphe Boulanger; even Romeo and Juliet, if we believe Shakespeare's hints that had they actually set up house together in Mantua, the result would have been something of a car crash.

Giving more cause for concern – for literature does dramatize for the sake of a good yarn – there's little scientific research showing a link between short-term attraction and long-term compatibility; Arthur Aron himself points out that while the closeness produced in his studies is similar to romantic passion, 'it seems unlikely that the procedure produces . . . commitment.' 'In love' might turn into a loss-leader for something deeper, but there's no absolute correlation between the two.

There is, however, correlation between 'in love' and anxiety. Here's another Arthur Aron experiment, this one involving eighty-five male subjects and a wobbly footbridge. Result: the men were significantly more likely to be charmed by a female researcher if they'd previously been scared out of their wits crossing the deep canyon at Capilano, Vancouver. (In case you're suspecting gender bias here, the experiment was replicated some years later with women as subjects and male researchers; it produced the same outcome.) What both groups experienced was a dynamic that's classic in the early stages of a relationship; our whole body is in a peak state of nervous tension, not only from wanting our beloved but also as a result of not knowing whether our beloved will want us. This arousal then provides the motivation to do exactly what we are genetically programmed to do, cling on to each other. Even the most delightful bonding involves some level of anxiety, and, in turn, anxiety often leads to bonding.

You can probably see where I'm going with this. We can easily confuse the strong emotion of the 'in love' kind with the strong emotion of more unhappy kinds. We may even find ourselves likely to bond in *any* uncertain situation, with any uncertain partner – one who is emotionally unreliable ('I'll phone you' syndrome), one who is seriously uninterested ('s/he's just not into you' syndrome), one who is terminally unavailable ('it's complicated' syndrome). In fact, when we keep choosing unsatisfying partners, that might be not despite the fact but *because* of the fact that they are unsatisfying. If you recognize yourself in this scenario, don't self-blame; there's a very small distinction between an emotional roller coaster that makes us squeal with delight and one that makes us shriek with horror, and most of us at some time choose the wrong ride.

The earthquake of love

There's something else we need to remember about 'in love'. It's date-stamped. That original flurry of addicted monoamines will in the end give way to a lower-key flow of the 'cuddle hormone' oxytocin, designed to give us a more secure connection and get us not just pushing the pram but setting up house and home until the kids have grown and flown. There's a natural switch from high arousal to low-key stability, from excitement to steadiness, from absolute adoration to loving respect: as Louis de Bernières writes in his novel *Captain Corelli's Mandolin*, 'a temporary madness . . . an earthquake . . . then it subsides.'

Given this non-correlation between 'in love' and compatibility, it's therefore wise to avoid making choices from the earthquake zone, wise to wait until the earth has stopped moving before we pitch permanent camp. As de Bernières suggests, at that point there is a decision to be made about whether we are so compatible, so committed that even without 'in love' we want to stay together. This stage beyond 'in love' may not feel as intensely exciting, but it's what makes a relationship stay the course. 'Love itself,' says de Bernières, 'is what is left over, when being in love has burned away.' If we want a partner for the long term, we need to discover what is 'left over'.

Here's an exercise to help in the discovery. Pick three friends you've known for a while and are emotionally at ease with. Now think of what makes them your friends; think of what you get from them that has maintained your connection over time. Fix in your mind that feeling of being comfortable with them, relaxed in their company, authentically yourself, simply content. And there's your point of reference, the touchstone to use when you fall in love. If you feel with a partner that same sense of comfort, relaxation, contentment – and if you sense that feeling could endure – then you are on safe ground.

Good navigation

Which unfortunately doesn't mean that the ground will stay safe for ever. Yes, we're always told that when we love we will not only live 'happily' but will do so 'ever after'. We're assured that, apart from when it's absent, denied or ended, 'love is a many-splendoured thing', 'love lifts us up where we belong', 'all you need is love'. And so we tend to set our compass for partner choice by the pole star of joy . . .

Often, that's good navigation. If we choose a partner who complements us, who completes our jigsaw and adds their skills and strengths to the ones we lack, we'll live a more effective but also a more contented life. In Jane Austen's *Pride and Prejudice*, Elizabeth Bennet, having spent most of the novel thinking that Darcy is 'the last man on earth' she would marry, realizes at last – and possibly too late – just how complementary they are and how happy their relationship could be. 'It was a union that must have been to the advantage of both; by her ease and liveliness, his mind might have been softened, his manners improved; and from his judgement, information, and knowledge of the world, she must have received benefit of greater importance.' (If you've never read the book, be reassured: they get together in the end.)

Similarly, if we choose a partner who supports us, who by their attention and responsiveness heals our emotional wounds and makes us whole, we'll live a more fulfilled but also a more joyful life. Here is another Elizabeth, this time Elizabeth Barrett, writing to fellow poet Robert Browning after he has expressed his love for her: 'To receive such a proof of attachment from you not only overpowers every present evil, but seems to me a full and abundant amends for the merely personal sufferings of my whole life. [My tears] went away in the moisture of new, happy tears. Henceforward I am yours.' (If you don't know the history, they married; he then helped her to not only bear lifelong illness and a family estrangement, but also fulfil her promise as a writer.)

People-growing

But despite these examples, love doesn't make us happy all the time and every time. Maybe an adorable partner has a less-than-lovable phase, an easy relationship starts to feel like hard work, a future that was glorious slowly becomes ordinary or even disagreeable. In Dickens's novel, David Copperfield finds it hard to come to terms with Dora's naivety and impracticality, while David Beckham's marriage has reportedly not been without its ups and downs. Faced with dissatisfaction, it's not surprising that we start to question our judgement. Does our unhappiness mean we chose the wrong partner? And what does it mean about how we made our decision and whether we should renege?

Here's the thing. A relationship is what psychologist David Schnarch, in his book *Passionate Marriage*, calls a 'people-growing process'. It invites us to flourish by learning to overcome not just the problems of everyday life, but the specific problems that our partner and our partnership present. It invites us to step up to the challenge of becoming more tolerant, more patient, more loving than we were before, in order to cope with the one we love. (If this seems unfair, be reassured. It cuts both ways; a partner has to step up in order to cope with us.)

This challenge of people-growing is never going to be a constantly happy one. It can't be. Poet David Whyte, in his work *The Three Mar-*

riages, offers the metaphor of buying two houses in order to join them together – but instead of being able to simply knock down the walls, we have to demolish both houses completely so we can rebuild, and 'from the razed foundations of our former individual [selves] make a new home'. Schnarch picks up on this metaphor but with an extra emotional challenge: that in order to do this we must become more loving not only to our partner, but to ourselves as well. We must be strong, self-contained, 'secure', comfortable in our own skin – for we need to feel 'at home' in ourselves in order to have 'a good place to invite a spouse to visit'.

Standing in love

Both Whyte and Schnarch say the same – that this process is universal, that it is a good thing, that we need to welcome it as a way of maturing and developing, that long-term it will lead to happiness because it will help us thrive. Similarly, Erich Fromm, whom we met earlier in this book, says that falling in love is inevitably followed by a period of needing to 'stand' in love, if our relationship is to survive. Happiness will not necessarily be what marks progress; sometimes there will be pain.

A common response to all this is to swallow hard as one tries to come to terms with the shock revelation that even the most successful 'love, sweet love' doesn't always feel so sweet. But there often follows a sigh of relief that relationship problems don't imply that the partners are wrong for each other or that they necessarily need to separate. For even if we make the most perfect partner-pick in the world, we will at some point meet challenges. We will always be required to master the essential human balancing act of trying to answer our own needs while meeting those of our beloved, of loving ourselves while loving another, and of growing through that process.

So the key aim in finding the right partner should not be to try to avoid that balancing act – it's inevitable – but to find someone for whose sake we'll attempt the act because we love them so much, someone who loves us so much that they'll make the attempt for our sake. The question for both sides becomes how to choose a partner who is so compelling that we're willing to demolish our own house in order to rebuild a more beautiful mutual home.

Diamond-polishing

The good news is that we likely know how to choose correctly even when we're not doing so deliberately. For humans are drawn towards those who help them grow; the message from Whyte, Schnarch and Fromm is that partner choice is the way we actively, though often unconsciously, choose to mature. Schnarch even likens it to the meeting of two flawless but rough diamonds that rub away every part of themselves that doesn't fit in order to stay joined together. The end result is not only a loving relationship, but two sparkling jewels.

So, for example, we may be drawn to someone who needs something from us that we find it hugely difficult to deliver: attention even when they are angry, energy even when we are drained, emotional control in the face of difficult circumstances. Over time, because we care, we learn to step up and meet these challenges – and in this way develop a part of ourselves we would otherwise never have developed.

Or, we may pair with someone who – once the rose-coloured glasses are off – manifests some vulnerability or fault that we dislike, or even deny, in ourselves. Because love means we are motivated to understand and accept that partner, we learn to accept and understand our own vulnerabilities – and so we thrive.

More unexpected, perhaps – for more explanation of this, reread Chapter 3 – we may find someone whose personality reflects that of someone from our early past with whom we've had a complicated relationship. That reflection may make our current relationship complicated – but given that we are now older and more mature, we may learn to relate to our partner in a way we never could to the original. We may grow up sufficiently to create a happy ending this time round.

Take some time to think back to past relationships with partners (or friends, or family) where things were challenging but left you changed for the better, even in small ways. You've almost certainly, in those relationships, chosen to be with people who helped you with the diamond-polishing. So what did those relationships give you? What benefits have you gained? And what can you learn that will help you begin – and maintain – your future partnership?

The right order

How can we tell whether a partner will help us mature in these ways and whether we can help them in return? There's no formula, no guaranteed way of discovering if someone constitutes our growth opportunity – and as with attachment tendencies, real evidence may only be possible when the relationship's well beyond the point of first choosing.

But in the earlier going, certain signs are encouraging: feeling ourselves becoming more emotionally truthful, and seeing our partner becoming equally more authentic; feeling encouraged by them to reach our potential, and being able to encourage them to do the same; finding ourselves both learning and teaching, like Elizabeth Bennet; or finding ourselves emotionally healing and professionally achieving, like Elizabeth Barrett. In her novel *Beloved*, the author Toni Morrison describes this kind of personal development as if the person in question were a jumble of jigsaw pieces, taken up by a partner, rearranged and returned 'in all the right order'. If we have chosen well, both partners may find their 'pieces' falling into place.

The sparkle

The lesson of this chapter is not that we should choose a partner with whom things are tough from the very beginning – if that's what's going on, it's not the right relationship. The lesson is that the best love is a three-part process, with the initial delights driving us on to ride out the medium-term challenges for the sake of long-term rewards. To complete the stories with which we began this chapter, David and Victoria Beckham are near to celebrating two decades together, while David Copperfield learned to accept his wife's failings and so allowed his marriage to gain stability, even if it was cut short by Dora's death.

Enough, then, of any alarm bells. My original statement of belief in love still stands, and more. Because, first, whether or not a relationship lasts, being love-struck may be worth it just for the experience. And, second, if the relationship does last, love-struck is a wonderful place to start. The very fact we are so drawn to someone else – the lure of the obsession – is a huge motivator to stay loyal if things become challenging. The fact that we want so much from a partner means we're driven to deliver in return. The fact that 'falling in love' means we bond, connect, open up, reveal and respond to each other emotionally creates the foundation for 'standing in love' further down the line. If what's left after the earthquake subsides is a solid core of commitment, then we have the best of both worlds.

So let's embrace the romance, let's enjoy the passion. In short, bring on the sparkle.

8. Knowing

Seven years would be insufficient to make some people acquainted with each other, and seven days are more than enough for others.

(Jane Austen, *Sense and Sensibility*)

The question we're most likely to ask ourselves when we begin to date is 'How will I know?' What this really implies is two questions, 'how' and 'when': 'How and when will I know enough to choose this person, or to not choose them, or to decide that the moment of choice is past?' Let me say from the start that there's no answer here, nor are there guarantees that one ever will know. All we can do is explore the possibilities.

Instant reaction

Possibility number one is that the answer to 'how will I know?' is 'sheer gut reaction' and the answer to 'when will I know?' is 'instantly'. Eyes meet across a crowded room and the deal is sealed; as examples, see two separate if very different American presidents. In his memoirs,

Bill Clinton reports that when his wife Hillary first spoke to him, he was so overwhelmed that he forgot his own name. Lyndon B. Johnson apparently asked 'Lady Bird', as his wife was known, for a date within minutes of meeting, and proposed at the end of that first date; they were still happily wed when he died almost forty years later.

Of course, an instant and instinctive decision about partner suitability is often a vote against – the elimination principle at work. Which is why, if all other boxes are ticked, it's often wise to follow up even the most disastrous first meeting with a replay. That allows us to gather more, and more accurate, evidence – as well as reducing self-consciousness on both sides, allowing prospective partners to shine. This advice was passed on to me by a colleague who judged her blind date to be socially incompetent but gave him the benefit of a second hearing. She soon discovered he was simply overawed by her, a trait which soon transformed itself into socially competent adoration on both sides.

Then there's the opposite danger. Over-speedy decisions can lead to being totally swept off one's feet by beauty and charm, only to real-

ize that one's given house-room to a monster.
That said, as I've confessed, I'm no enemy of a
little carefully managed infatuation. And the
danger's often resolved by the inevitable removal
of rose-coloured glasses – inevitable because
such instant passion is likely to implode at the
first sniff of a problem; as Shakespeare put it,
'These violent delights have violent ends / . . .
like fire and powder / Which as they kiss, con-
sume.' But if instant enchantment makes us
want to instantly commit in some comparatively
irreversible way (mortgage, marriage, moth-
erhood) then it's best to apply the necessary
brakes.

Taking time

Bill Clinton may have been so overwhelmed by
Hillary that his brain stopped working, but the
'how' of knowing is normally more thoughtful.
And it's usual to take longer than Lyndon Johnson's few minutes to decide that we have found
our life partner; radioactivity pioneer Marie Cu-
rie, for instance, turned down husband Pierre's
proposals a full seven times before she was convinced. Taking at least some time, space and

consideration typically works best because it helps us to discover more about a partner, allows them to discover more about us. Where possible, dig deeper, search wider, allow both logic and emotion, head and heart to synchronize. As the Russian proverb runs, 'Trust, but verify'.

Which is why communities have traditionally built in delay: long engagements, no sex before marriage, betrothal for a year and a day before the wedding proper, all so we can verify the information and draw a considered conclusion. Our contemporary speedy courtship rituals – sleeping together without vows, moving in together without documentation – are only acceptable because we're now not bound together for life if love turns to hate. Ironically, the most modern method, online dating, has reintroduced some of that traditional delay, with users going through a sometimes lengthy and in-depth process of 'getting to know you' while they continue to 'get to know' several others online until they commit.

But it's also best not to be too slow and too considered, for there are dangers in hesitation; we may lose not only momentum but also faith.

Especially in the key transition stages – having sex, becoming monogamous, moving in – if the moment passes, so too may the belief that it was a good idea. If you're worried about a timetable be reassured that, as the Jane Austen quotation at the beginning of this chapter shows, there is no ideal. That said, as very rough guidelines, two months of regular dating is long enough to know whether both sides want to declare themselves partners, two years long enough to know whether lifetime commitment is possible. Pass those breakpoints and it's justifiable to question the length of the journey.

How do you know?

So take stock. What is your journey to knowing? Do you rush into connection, physical or emotional, with spontaneous eagerness, enthusiasm and a marked inability either to doubt or to tolerate delayed gratification? Or do you progress so slowly and serenely in affairs of the heart that onlookers – or even the objects of your affection themselves – believe you're ambivalent? In other words, do you typically push for commitment because you're so quickly convinced that you've found perfection, or delay it because you're waiting for perfection to prove itself?

There is an argument here for acting against usual tendencies. Previous speedy commitment may have led to some lack of judgement, previous tardy commitment may have meant losing love. And, as the old saying goes, 'If you always do what you've always done, you'll get what you've always got.' So if we normally rush in, then, without playing 'treat 'em mean and keep 'em keen', we could maybe try holding back on that first kiss, that first sexual encounter, that first meeting with parents, until we know precisely what we're dealing with. Conversely, if we typically tend to hesitate, then, without playing 'wear your heart on your sleeve', we could maybe 'lean in' to suggesting that date, supplying that extra front-door key, declaring those intentions – even before it feels completely comfortable. Altering approach is, as always, a challenge. But perhaps if you do what you've never done, you might get what you've never before got.

One of the nicest, as well as one of the most effective, ways to make a partnership decision – which involves taking time to explore but doesn't drag things out – was suggested by my col-

league Dr Charley Ferrer. Its approach is based
not so much on information-gathering or tim-
ing as on attitude. For ninety days, Dr Ferrer
advises, we should commit completely. We
shouldn't hold back for fear of being taken for
granted, shouldn't cling on for fear of being
rejected. Instead, for a full three months, we
should offer full engagement in giving and taking, full emotional responsiveness, full trust
that the partnership will continue. In other
words, we should behave as if we already 'know'
and have already chosen. If after that time we
have no hesitations, then we know enough to
say a completely wholehearted 'yes'. If at the end
of the ninety days we are still hesitating, we have
gained more than enough knowledge to justify
a 'no'.

Saying no

In some cases that 'no' is obvious. Deceit. Infi-
delity. Drug dependency. Abuse. Violence. All
these bad behaviours are perfectly good reasons
to flee, even after making an initial choice.

There can also be good reason to flee when
there's no bad behaviour at all. There are

numerous partner combinations that don't augur well: deal-breakers in our preferences; differing values, goals, personalities; questions about one's enjoyment of a partner's company; a not-quite-good-enough sex life; an annoying level of conflict (even if it is generally bearable). As Ross from the TV comedy *Friends* commented when asked why he and lesbian Carol weren't together: 'This is not a mix-and-match situation', and we shouldn't attempt to make round holes accommodate square pegs. (We equally, of course, shouldn't simply walk away in an attempt to force the pegs into the holes; break-up rarely works as a way to compel commitment in ourselves or others, and even if we reconcile, such abandonment will always strain the partnership, sometimes irreversibly.)

Sometimes too, the answer is neither to go nor to stay but to try the third alternative. Change. If the benefits of partnership are obvious, we could – kindly, supportively, specifically – ask for the adjustments we want. Our partner might then answer – willingly, readily, enthusiastically – that they're happy to oblige. Or vice versa. If that's the conversation, there's good reason to stay.

The bad news is that, without that conversation, there's every reason to go. Professor Ted Huston's fourteen-year couple study, mentioned earlier in this book, found that when women in the courting phase of a relationship predict future problems, their predictions usually come true. So if we decide to stay with someone in the hope they'll improve in time, we're not really committing to the person they are now but to a future ideal that's highly improbable. As Albert Einstein – who was something of a philosopher as well as a theoretical physicist – famously commented, 'Men marry women with the hope they will never change. Women marry men with the hope they will change. Invariably they are both disappointed.'

If having done due diligence we still feel a quiver of doubt, we could stay one more day to make absolutely sure. But if what we feel at the thought of staying is a flinch, a nausea, an exhaustion, that's our unconscious screaming 'go'. In which case, let me offer you an absolving 'get out of jail free' card. It is fine to turn someone down. In fact, it's actually best to turn them down if you have come to the conclusion that they aren't for you. Because by walking away you're not just freeing yourself to find someone you can love. You are also freeing your no-longer-potential partner to find someone who can love them. Don't feel guilty. If we know our heart is not in a relationship we do right by everyone if we leave.

Not being chosen

Sometimes, though, the situation's more complex. Our heart is in, fully in. But our feelings aren't returned – or perhaps worse, not returned right now but with a hint that they might be at some future time. Then things become hugely more difficult – though this is also a timeless theme in our history and culture. The poet Dante's love for Beatrice. The Hunchback of Notre Dame's longing for Esmeralda. Mark in *Love Actually* standing before his ideal (but already happily married) partner with a poster reading 'my wasted heart will love you'. These tales touch us – and not only because we prefer a good ending to our love stories but also because they trigger a human terror that began when we were born: that we will not get everything we want in life.

However unfulfilled a relationship – Dante loved Beatrice for life, but only met her twice –

not being chosen is a blow. If, or when, it happens to us, we shouldn't underestimate the impact; studies have equated this loss to an actual physical attack, a trauma, a bereavement. Then we need to cling to the fact that – given some weeping and wailing, but also given time, human support and a sense of perspective – we will likely move through the suffering.

But if we don't move through rejection, we can land in deep trouble. For sometimes the label 'non-available' spurs us to even more commitment; surely if we can be different, woo more successfully, offer more resources, deliver more favours or simply try harder, we will get what we want.

Here the cautionary tale from literature is the Great Gatsby, F. Scott Fitzgerald's millionaire hero who invests everything he has in trying to rekindle the love of Daisy Buchanan's 'beautiful little fool'. He takes a luxurious mansion directly across the bay from her marital home, spends endless nights staring over at the green light at the end of her dock, throws hugely extravagant parties to tempt her to come to him.

It's clear from the start that there will be no happy ending here; Daisy's self-absorption

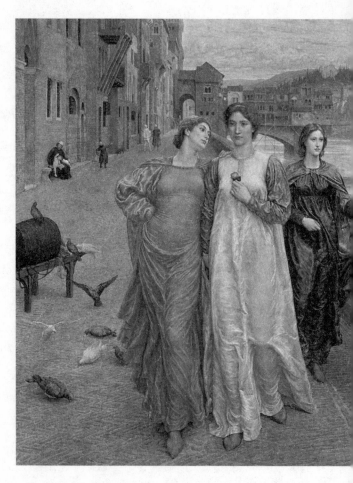

Dante and Beatrice. Sometimes, there's nothing more comfortable than focussing our choice on a prospect who, because we will never have them, will never disappoint us or be disappointed by us.

makes it almost inevitable that, while she does restart her affair with Gatsby, she will in the end abandon him. But Gatsby himself creates his own tragedy by sacrificing all to win the love of someone who cannot truly love him, squandering his fortune in relentless decadence, abandoning his values and in the end losing his life to protect Daisy. The whole story is shot through with the pointlessness of clinging on in hope.

If our love story ever approaches that of Gatsby, the answer is not to twist our hearts and our souls out of shape as he did, but conversely to be even more authentic than usual. If after a while we are still not loved, then however much we mourn, it's been a lucky escape. In the same way as it's best to free up a partner we don't want, it is also best to be freed from a partner who doesn't want us. We deserve more than that.

Being chosen

What if, instead, we are adored without adoring in return? If our immediate reaction to being picked is obvious repulsion, that's fairly straight-

forward; there likely follows a few embarrass-
ing conversations, a little self-reproach and the
occasional need to repel the boarder in question.

More difficult is when our reaction is not repulsion but temptation. For being the object of
desire can be highly seductive. If we suffer the
normal human tendency to self-negation, it may
feel very good indeed when someone else puts
us at the centre of their universe, giving us a
control over them that's even more seductive
because we aren't in any danger of ceding any
control to them. (Plus, if we are feeling pessi-
mistic because previous partner choices have
misfired, such a person may be even more attractive because we believe they are our only re-
maining option.)

Given all this, being pursued can make us
blind to danger signals. We may ignore huge
signs of incompatibility, consign huge doubts to
the file marked 'ignore'. And, particularly if
our would-be partner stays the course, we
may stay with them despite misgivings; there is
something deeply romantic about Being Won
Despite All Challenges. 'She wanted me even
though she was married . . .'; 'I wasn't inter-
ested but he was so keen . . .'; 'I was convinced
by her conviction that I was the one for her . . .'

It was Wallis Simpson who – feeling bound to marry the abdicated Edward VIII long after she had tired of him – commented: 'You have no idea how hard it is to live out a great romance.'

Balance, imbalance

Again, pause and take stock. Do you recognize in yourself a habit of staying in a relationship well beyond the point you should be leaving? Of leaving when you should be giving it another chance? Are you consistently drawn to those who don't pick you? To those who are married – whether to spouse or to job? To those who care, but only at certain times, only in certain situations and only when you offer attention, support or no-strings sex?

Or do you find yourself in relationships with partners who do choose you but who you know, heart of hearts, will make you deeply unhappy? Do you find yourself persuaded by intensity (or by flattery, or by genuine if one-sided love), to the point of ignoring your own doubts and ending in uneasy partnership? In all these situations, it may be time to change.

All that said, don't panic if there's some imbalance in a relationship, particularly at the start. Every relationship suffers disequilibrium. Even for just a few moments, one person wonders while the other is certain; one person doubts while the other has faith. So long as the dynamic eventually settles into an equal match, that's fine. More, if what we experience at the start of a promising relationship is a certain deliberation on either side, this may well be good news. The resulting choice, if it comes, is likely to be more considered – and therefore more dependable.

Choosing

The first chapter of this book painted partner choice as a journey – and the promise that description offers is that there is a conclusion to the trip. It's a promise that will almost certainly come true. We may have encountered detours or cul-de-sacs along the way, but the vast majority of us will reach our destination. We will let go of alternative possibilities and begin to focus more and more surely on one. We will come to a point where we believe that we can love, and that we can be loved in return.

And there we are, decision made. We echo the moving words of poet Edwin Muir: 'yours, my love, is the right human face'. We know. We have committed. We are set for the happiest of endings.

Except, except . . . of course this isn't the end. Commitment is only the beginning, the first choice. There will be other decisions to come and it's wise to remember they are out there waiting for us.

Moving in together. Getting engaged. Marrying. Having children. Raising those children and then staying together to the end of life. The thing about these later transitions is that by the time we make them, we're in a different place from before. As Somerset Maugham pointed out, we are not the same as we were even a year ago, and 'nor are those we love'.

Through the course of our relationship, we will likely several times come slap up against what can only be described as the Wall of Life – trials of illness, accident, job change, ageing, bereavement. Through these, and with the passing of time, we will learn more about our partner and they will learn more about us. And this may shift the goalposts. Soberingly, the second half of the Somerset Maugham quota-

tion reminds us that it is only good fortune
if 'we, changing, continue to love a changed
person'.

Whether or not we have such good fortune,
much of what this book suggests is always
relevant. In the context not of a hoped-for or
recent connection but an existing and lengthy
commitment, it is still useful to specify what
we want from our partnership; to reassess the
fit with our partner's values, goals and personality; to face fully whether we can still emotionally respond to each other. And sometimes that
raises questions. If our partner promised us a
rose garden but over the years has delivered
only armfuls of brutally stinging nettles, it's
understandable if we dump the greenery in the
waste bin and head for the door.

Nettles aside, the most important factor in
making future partnership decisions – just as
for the initial choice to partner with that person –
is not whether we are currently ecstatic but
whether we are currently growing, whether we
trust that we will grow in the future, and whether
we believe our partner is growing too. If we are
in a relationship that pushes us to mature,
we may not be 100 per cent joyful, 24/7 – ask
any caterpillar in the process of becoming a

butterfly. Yet if we are still evolving, that will make it worthwhile to keep loyal.

Let me end with a tribute to continuing loyalty. In his novel *Love in the Time of Cholera*, Gabriel García Márquez describes the experience of the multitude of ordinary couples who stay the course even though it proves hard. He pays tribute to the immense courage and willingness of those who have chosen again, beyond the first romantic decision, who have overcome the challenges of 'daily incomprehension', 'instantaneous hatred' and 'reciprocal nastiness' that characterize most relationships, and he celebrates that it is fully possible to come through and to triumph, to reach the point where partners 'love each other best'.

That's the hope. That if both of us keep evolving, keep learning, keep growing, then at some point in the future, we will be able to create a wonderful partnership, to relate to each other as never before, to love each other 'best'. And then we will know for absolute certain that we have made the right choice.

Bibliography

Books

Louisa May Alcott, *Little Women*, Vintage Children's Classics, 2012 edn

Jane Austen, *Pride and Prejudice*, Wordsworth Classics, 1992 edn

——, *Sense and Sensibility*, Wordsworth Classics, 1992 edn

Louis de Bernières, *Captain Corelli's Mandolin*, Vintage, 1998

Emily Brontë, *Wuthering Heights*, Wordsworth Classics, 1992 edn

Brené Brown, *Daring Greatly*, Avery Publishing Group, 2015

Gary Chapman, *The Five Love Languages*, Moody Press, 2015

Stephanie Coontz, *Marriage, a History: How Love Conquered Marriage*, Penguin USA, 2006

Helen Fielding, *Bridget Jones's Diary*, Picador, 2001

F. Scott Fitzgerald, *The Great Gatsby*, Wordsworth Classics, 1992 edn

Gustave Flaubert, *Madame Bovary*, Wordsworth Classics, 1993 edn

Erich Fromm, *The Art of Loving*, Thorsons, 2010

Elizabeth Gilbert, *Eat, Pray, Love*, Bloomsbury, 2007

Dr Sue Johnson, *Hold Me Tight*, Piatkus, 2011

——, *Love Sense*, Little, Brown, 2013

Daniel Kahneman, *Thinking Fast and Slow*, Penguin, 2012

Claire Langhamer, *The English in Love: The Intimate Story of an Emotional Revolution*, OUP, 2013

Gabriel García Márquez, *Love in the Time of Cholera*, Vintage, 2007

Simon May, *Love: A History*, Yale University Press, 2012

Chris McKinlay, *Optimal Cupid: Mastering the Hidden Logic of OkCupid*, CreateSpace, 2014

Toni Morrison, *Beloved*, Vintage Classics, 2007 edn

David Schnarch, *Passionate Marriage: Keeping Love and Intimacy Alive in Committed Relationships*, W. W. Norton, 2009

William Shakespeare, *Romeo and Juliet*, Wordsworth Classics, 2000 edn

Leo Tolstoy, *Anna Karenina*, Wordsworth Classics, 1995 edn

Amy Webb, *Data, a Love Story*, Plume, 2014

David Whyte, *The Three Marriages: Reimagining Work, Self and Relationship*, Riverhead Books, 2010

Jeanette Winterson, *Written on the Body*, Vintage, 1993

Websites and other resources

www.notimeforlove.com

Eli J. Finkel et al., 'Online Dating: A Critical Analysis From the Perspective of Psychological Science', available at www.psychologicalscience.org

www.quantifiedbreakup.tumblr.com

The School of Life, 100 Questions: Love Edition (100 question cards with box – a toolkit for relationships)

The School of Life offers coaching and therapy for relationship enhancement: www.theschooloflife .com/london/shop/therapy/life-coaching

In Britain you can also find counsellors through the College of Sexual and Relationship Therapists: www.cosrt.org.uk, the British Association for Counselling and Psychotherapy: www.itsgoodtotalk.org.uk and Relate: www.relate.org.uk.

Acknowledgements

My thanks go to everyone who has made this book possible, especially my agent Barbara Levy and all the staff at the School of Life and at Pan Macmillan, especially Morgwn Rimel, Cindy Chan, Robin Harvie, Zennor Compton, Laura Carr, Marcia Mihotich and Jonathan Baker, all of whom have been endlessly helpful. Above all, my thanks go to Caroline Brimmer, who originally invited me to help her develop the 'How to Choose a Partner' course at the School of Life, and whose talent, insight and support have been an inspiration; without Caroline, this book would not have happened.

Photographic Credits

The author and publisher would like to thank the following for permission to reproduce the images used in this book:

Page 2 *The Arnolfini Portrait* © Thaliastock / Mary Evans

Pages 8–9 *Sir Galahad – the Quest of the Holy Grail*, 1870 (oil on canvas), Hughes, Arthur (1832–1915) © Walker Art Gallery, National Museums Liverpool / Bridgeman Images

Pages 22–23 Traffic Sign With Heart Shape © Richard Newstead / Getty Images

Page 35 Human Heart Map © Kate Hiscock / Getty Images

Pages 50–51 Come Through © Everett Collection / REX Shutterstock

Page 56 Watching the Roulette Wheel, Hollywood, California, 1930 (b/w photo) ©Underwood Archives / UIG / Bridgeman Images

Page 61 Scene at Reelfoot Lake © Andreas Feininger / Getty Images

Page 64 Jam and Marmalade aisle, Woolworths store, 1956 (b/w photo), English Photographer, (20th century) © Private Collection / Bridgeman Images

Pages 88–89 *West Side Story* Photo © Michael Ochs Archive / Getty Images

Page 94 A Man Hiking © Lambert / Getty Images

Page 103 Kissing Couple 1968 ©Mary Evans Picture Library / Shirley Baker

Pages 112–113 *The Creation of Adam* © Massimo Pizzotti / Getty Images

Page 133 Corkscrew © Keystone France / Getty Images

Pages 160–161 *Dante and Beatrice*, 1883 (oil on canvas), Holiday, Henry (1839–1927) © Walker Art Gallery, National Museums Liverpool / Bridgeman Images

Explore All of the "Maintenance Manuals for
the Mind" from the School of Life Library

How to Think More About Sex
Alain de Botton
ISBN 978-1-250-03065-8
E-ISBN 978-1-250-03066-5

How to Stay Sane
Philippa Perry
ISBN 978-1-250-03063-4
E-ISBN 978-1-250-03064-1

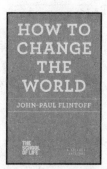

How to Find Fulfilling Work
Roman Krznaric
ISBN 978-1-250-03069-6
E-ISBN 978-1-250-03070-2

How to Change the World
John-Paul Flintoff
ISBN 978-1-250-03067-2
E-ISBN 978-1-250-03068-9

PICADOR
www.picadorusa.com

Available wherever books and e-books are sold.

Explore All of the "Maintenance Manuals for the Mind" from the School of Life Library

How to Be Alone
Sara Maitland
ISBN 978-1-250-05902-4
E-ISBN 978-1-250-05903-1

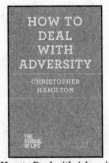

How to Deal with Adversity
Christopher Hamilton
ISBN 978-1-250-05900-0
E-ISBN 978-1-250-05901-7

How to Think About Exercise
Damon Young
ISBN 978-1-250-05904-8
E-ISBN 978-1-250-05905-5

How to Age
Anne Karpf
ISBN 978-1-250-05898-0
E-ISBN 978-1-250-05899-7

PICADOR

www.picadorusa.com

Available wherever books and e-books are sold.

Explore All of the "Maintenance Manuals for
the Mind" from the School of Life Library

How to Be a Leader
Martin Bjergegaard and Cosmina Popa
ISBN 978-1-250-07873-5
E-ISBN 978-1-250-07874-2

How to Think Like an Entrepeneur
Philip Delves Broughton
ISBN 978-1-250-07871-1
E-ISBN 978-1-250-07872-8

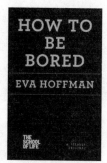

How to Be Bored
Eva Hoffman
ISBN 978-1-250-07867-4
E-ISBN 978-1-250-07868-1

How to Choose a Partner
Susan Quilliam
ISBN 978-1-250-07869-8
E-ISBN 978-1-250-07870-4

PICADOR

www.picadorusa.com

Available wherever books and e-books are sold.